Stopwatch

Teacher's Guide

2

Eric Zuarino

Richmond

Richmond
58 St Aldates
Oxford
OX1 1ST
United Kingdom

Stopwatch Teacher's Guide Level 2

First Edition: January 2016
Fifth Reprint: July 2019
ISBN: 978-607-06-1249-7

© Text: Eric Zuarino
© Richmond Publishing, S.A. de C.V. 2016
Av. Río Mixcoac No. 274, Col. Acacias,
Benito Juárez, C.P. 03240, Ciudad de México

Publisher: Justine Piekarowicz
Editorial Team: Suzanne Guerrero, Kimberly MacCurdy, Cara Norris, Joep van der Werff
Art and Design Coordinators: Jaime Angeles, Karla Avila
Design: Jaime Angeles, Karla Avila
Layout: Erick López, Daniel Mejía, Perla Zapien
Pre-Press Coordinator: Daniel Santillán
Pre-Press Team: Susana Alcántara, Virginia Arroyo, Daniel Santillán
Cover Design: Karla Avila
Cover Photograph: © **Thinkstock:** IPGGutenbergUKLtd (Young Woman Swimming in Pool)

All rights reserved. No part of this work may be reproduced, stored in a retrieval system or transmitted in any form or by any means without prior written permission from the Publisher.

Richmond publications may contain links to third party websites or apps. We have no control over the content of these websites or apps, which may change frequently, and we are not responsible for the content or the way it may be used with our materials. Teachers and students are advised to exercise discretion when accessing the links.

The Publisher has made every effort to trace the owner of copyright material; however, the Publisher will correct any involuntary omission at the earliest opportunity.

Printed in China

Contents

- 4   Scope and Sequence
- 6   Introduction to the Teacher's Guide
- 10   **Unit 0**   What are stereotypes?
- 15   **Unit 1**   Why are sports important?
- 29   **Unit 2**   How do you get around?
- 43   **Unit 3**   What makes a good friend?
- 57   **Unit 4**   What do we eat?
- 71   **Unit 5**   Why do we need a vacation?
- 85   **Unit 6**   What's your story?
- 99   **Unit 7**   How do we contribute?
- 113   **Unit 8**   How do we spend our free time?
- 126   CD1 and CD2 Contents
- 127   Verb List

Scope and Sequence

Unit	Vocabulary	Grammar	Skills
0 What are stereotypes?	**Review:** countries, nationalities, common verbs	Verb *be*; *There is / are*; Present continuous; Present simple; Prepositions of place: *at, behind, in, in front of, on, under*	**Reading:** Reading e-mails
1 Why are sports important?	**Sports:** baseball, basketball, cricket, cycling, football, rugby, soccer, swimming, tennis, table tennis **Adjectives:** active, big, dangerous, expensive, fast, heavy, modern, old, popular, strong, tall	Comparative and superlative adjectives	**Reading:** Knowing when to look up words **Writing:** Expressing opinions **Project:** Writing a sports manual
2 How do you get around?	**Places in a City:** bank, coffee shop, convenience store, drugstore, mall, park, school, supermarket **Transportation:** bike, bus, car, motorcycle, plane, subway, train	Imperatives; Irregular comparative and superlative adjectives	**Listening:** Following directions on a map **Reading:** Identifying the objective of a text **Project:** Writing a proposal
3 What makes a good friend?	**Physical Description:** blond, braces, chubby, glasses, long, medium height, medium weight, short, thin **Personality:** funny, intelligent, kind, outgoing, rude, serious, shy	Present simple; Present continuous	**Listening:** Identifying speaker's attitude **Writing:** Completing a form **Project:** Making a self-care kit
4 What do we eat?	**Food and Drinks:** apple, banana, beans, beef, bread, broccoli, butter, carrot, cheese, chicken, egg, fish, juice, milk, onions, oranges, pasta, rice, soda, water	Countable and uncountable nouns; Quantifiers: *some, any*	**Reading:** Identifying main ideas **Speaking:** Recommending a restaurant **Project:** Writing a healthy menu

Unit	Vocabulary	Grammar	Skills
5 Why do we need a vacation?	**Tourist Attractions:** amusement park, aquarium, art museum, beach, historic center, mountains, street market, zoo **Adjectives:** beautiful, boring, crowded, fun, great, noisy, terrible	Verb *be*: *was, were*	**Listening:** Predicting the information **Writing:** Making a vacation scrapbook **Project:** Making a podcast
6 What's your story?	**Movie and Book Genres:** autobiography, children's book, fantasy, romance; action, animated, comedy, science fiction **Adjectives:** boring, funny, sad, interesting, inspirational **Irregular Verbs:** found, made, met, saw, went, wrote	Past simple	**Listening:** Identifying sequence in a narrative **Writing:** Connecting ideas in a past-tense text **Project:** Making a timeline
7 How do we contribute?	**Professions:** artist, journalist, nurse, scientist, social worker **Workplaces:** community center, hospital, laboratory, office, studio	Past simple	**Reading:** Identifying the purpose: *persuade, inform, entertain* **Speaking:** Talking about a hero based on prompts **Project:** Solving a problem in the community
8 How do we spend our free time?	**Chores and Free-time Activities:** clean (your) room, do the dishes, do homework, go to the park, hang out with friends, play video games, take out the trash, walk the dog, watch a movie **Emotions:** angry, bored, excited, happy, nervous, sad, scared, tired	*Have to*; Future: *going to*	**Reading:** Reading for information **Speaking:** Inviting, accepting and rejecting an invitation **Project:** Carrying out and presenting a survey

The Concept

Stopwatch is a motivating, six-level secondary series built around the concept of visual literacy.

- *Stopwatch* constructs students' language skills from A0 to B1 of the Common European Framework of Reference (CEFR).
- A stopwatch symbolizes energy, speed, movement and competition and gives immediate feedback. The *Stopwatch* series offers dynamic, engaging activities and timed challenges that encourage students to focus and train for mastery.
- *Stopwatch* has a strong visual component to facilitate and deepen learning through authentic tasks, compelling images and the use of icons.
- The series was conceived for the international market, with a wide range of topics, incorporating cultures from around the world.
- The six-level framework of the series allows for different entry points to fit the needs of each school or group of students.
- The syllabus has been carefully structured. Each level recycles and expands on the language that was used in the previous books. This process of spiraled language development helps students internalize what they are learning.
- Each level of *Stopwatch* covers 90 – 120 hours of classroom instruction, plus an additional 20 hours of supplementary activities and materials in the Teacher's Guide and Teacher's Toolkit.

The Components

Student's Book & Workbook

Units are divided into distinct spreads, each with a clear focus:

- A **Big Question** establishes the central theme of the unit and promotes critical thinking, curiosity and interest in learning.
- **Vocabulary** is presented in thematic sets and with rich visual support to convey meaning.
- **Grammar** is introduced in context, enabling students to see the meaning, form and use of the structure.
- **Skills** (reading, listening, writing and speaking) are developed through engaging topics.
- **Culture** invites the learner to immerse oneself in the rich variety of cultures and peoples on our planet.
- **Review** activities provide consolidated practice for each of the grammar and vocabulary areas.
- In the **Project**, students apply the skills they learned in the unit to a creative task built around the Big Question.
- **Just for Fun** is a page with fun activities that teachers can assign to fast finishers.
- The **Workbook** pages offer extended practice with the vocabulary, structures and skills of the unit.
- **The Student's CD** contains all the listening material in the units.

Teacher's Guide

Brief instructions or summaries provide a quick guide for each Student's Book activity, including **answer keys** and **audio scripts**.

A fun and engaging **warm-up** activity reviews previous knowledge and prepares students for what will be seen in each lesson.

A **wrap-up** task practices newly-learned material. Warm-ups and wrap-ups usually take the form of games.

Extension tasks promote use of language in communication and real-life situations.

Digital options provide alternatives to the projects using electronic media.

Specific questions, related to the Big Question of the unit, stimulate critical thinking.

Teaching tips help develop and enrich teachers' skills.

Teacher's Toolkit (printable materials)

The Teacher's Toolkit is a comprehensive resource that is delivered in two CDs.

🔘 **CD1** includes the Class Audio and Worksheets

Worksheets
- Grammar Worksheets (2 per unit) with Answer Key
- Reading Worksheets (2 per unit) with Guidelines and Answer Key
- Vocabulary Worksheets (2 per unit) with Answer Key

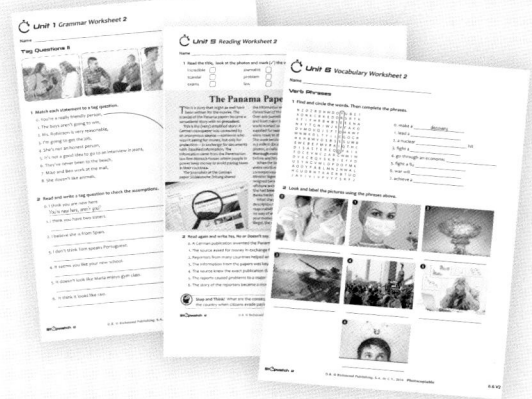

🔘 **CD2** includes Project Rubrics, Score Cards, Tests and Test Audios

Project Rubrics
- These contain proposed criteria that can be used to evaluate students' performance in the completion of the unit projects.

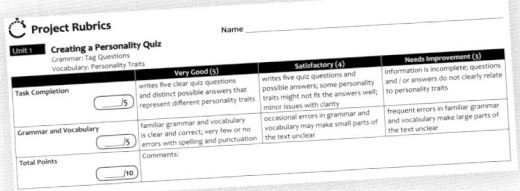

Scorecard
- These help students evaluate their progress by reflecting on their newly-acquired grammar, vocabulary, reading and listening skills.

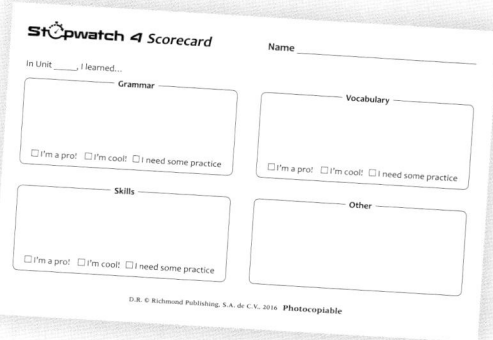

Tests

- **Placement Tests** (Beginner & Intermediate) with Grading Scale and Answer Key
  These will help teachers assess students' level of English on an individual and group basis and select appropriate tests.

- **Standard Tests** (1 per unit) with Answer Key
  These cover the vocabulary and grammar from the units, as well as reading and listening skills.
- **Tests Plus** (1 per unit) with Answer Key
  These are the **extended** version of the Standard Tests, which include an additional communication component designed to assess speaking and writing.

- **Mid-Term Tests** with Answer Key
  These should be given out after having completed U4.
- **Final Tests** with Answer Key
  These should be given out after having completed U8.

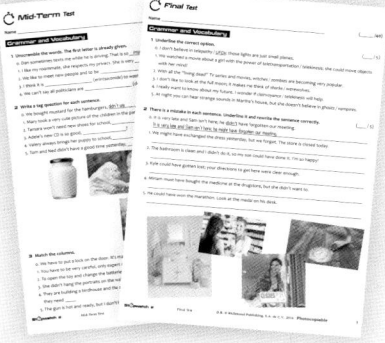

The Big Question: Why are sports important?

- **Student's Book & Workbook**

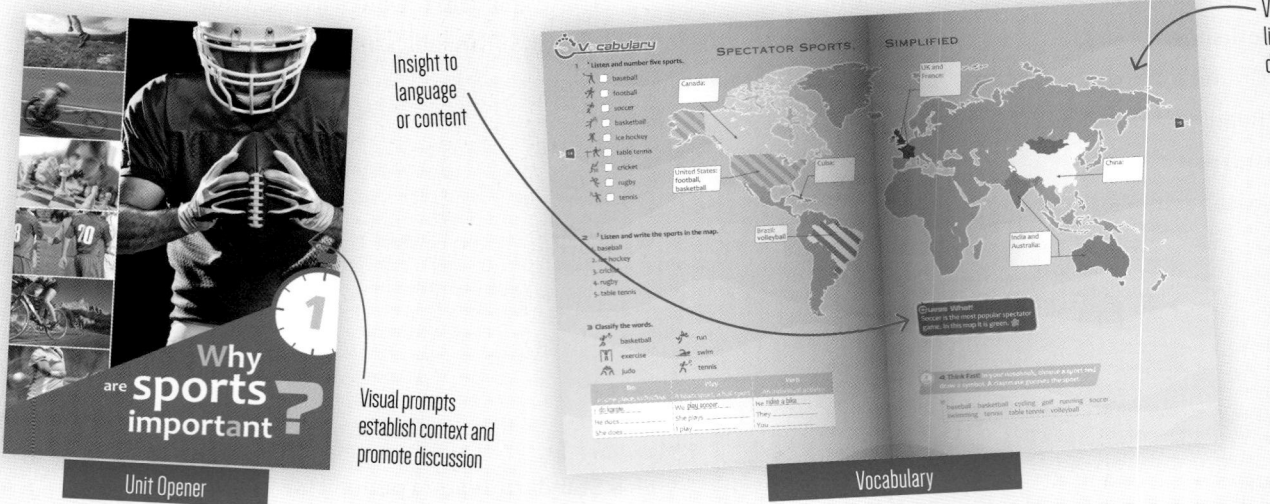

Unit Opener — Visual prompts establish context and promote discussion

Insight to language or content

Vocabulary — Visual literacy development

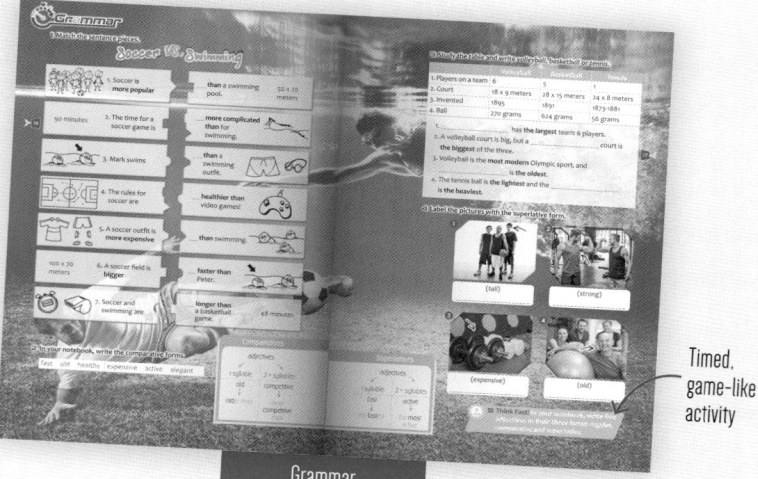

Grammar — Timed, game-like activity

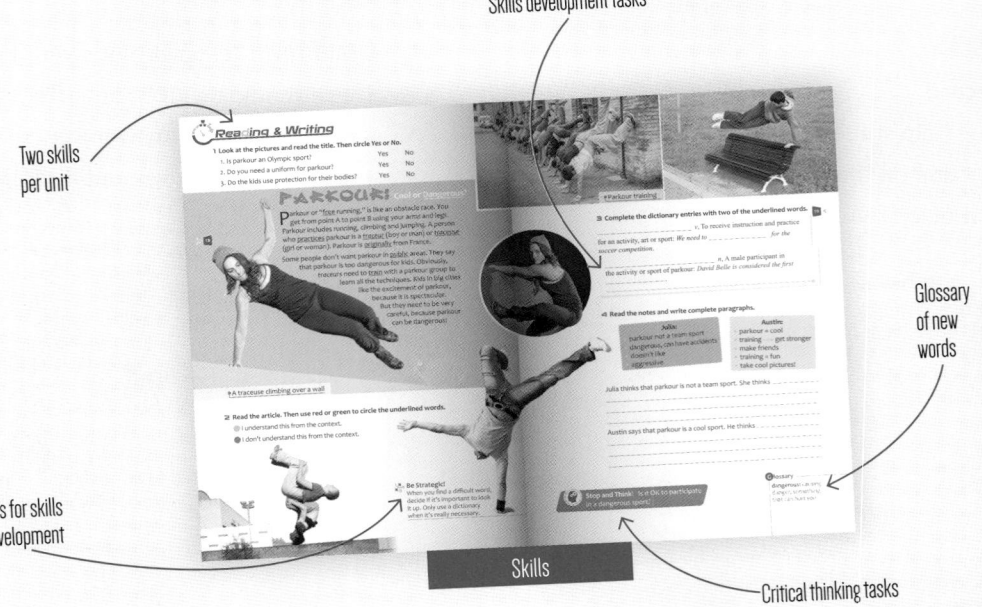

Skills — Two skills per unit · Tips for skills development · Skills development tasks · Glossary of new words · Critical thinking tasks

8

Student's Book & Workbook

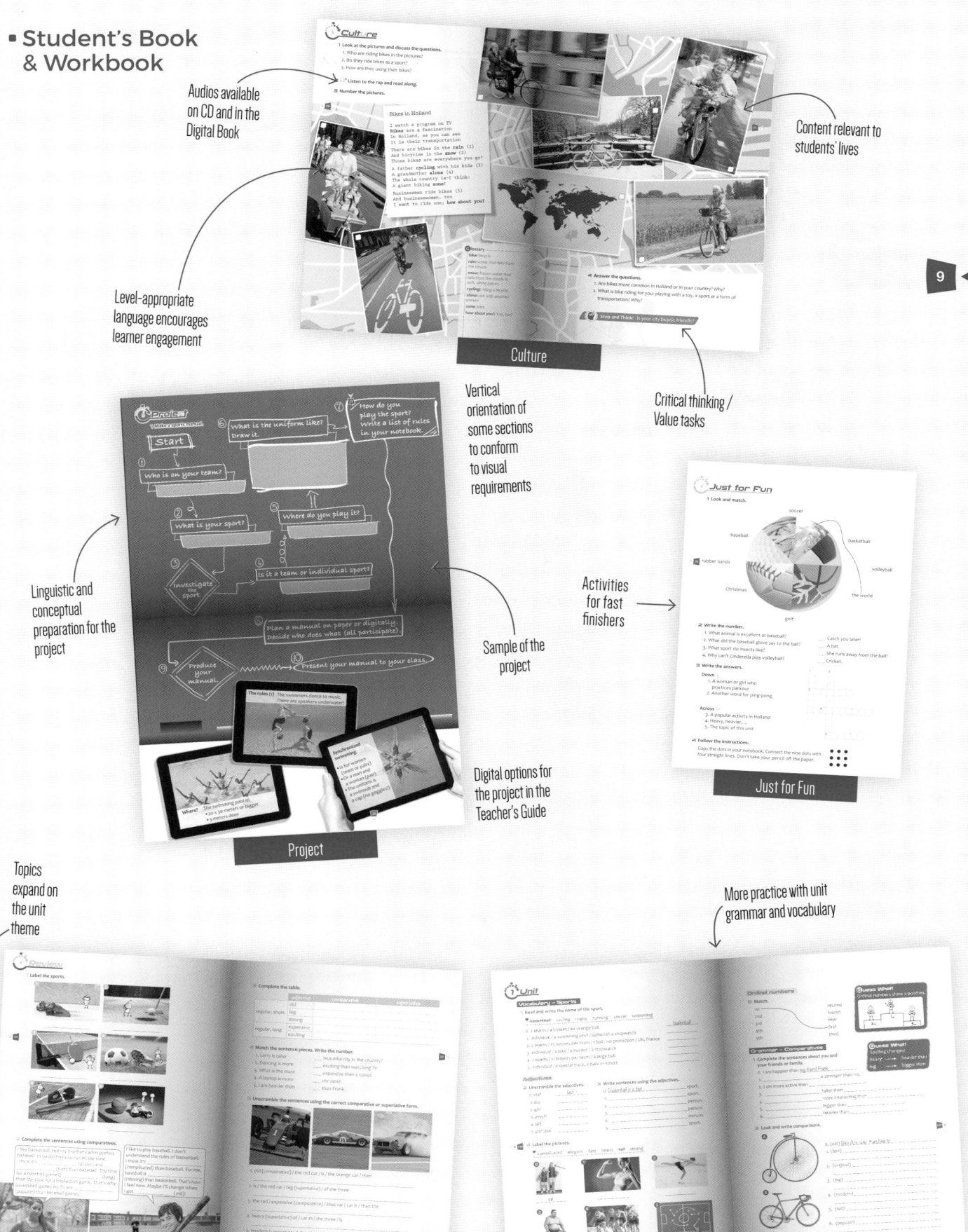

- Audios available on CD and in the Digital Book
- Level-appropriate language encourages learner engagement
- Content relevant to students' lives
- Critical thinking / Value tasks
- Culture
- Linguistic and conceptual preparation for the project
- Vertical orientation of some sections to conform to visual requirements
- Sample of the project
- Activities for fast finishers
- Just for Fun
- Digital options for the project in the Teacher's Guide
- Project
- Topics expand on the unit theme
- More practice with unit grammar and vocabulary
- Review
- Workbook section

What are stereotypes?

Grammar
Verb *be*: The people <u>are</u> happy.
There is / are: <u>There are</u> two children.
Present continuous: She <u>is writing</u> on the board.
Present simple: The singer <u>lives</u> in a small town.
Prepositions of place: *at, behind, in, in front of, on, under*: A man is sitting <u>on</u> a camel.

Reading
Reading e-mails

Vocabulary
Review: countries, nationalities, common verbs

▶ 10

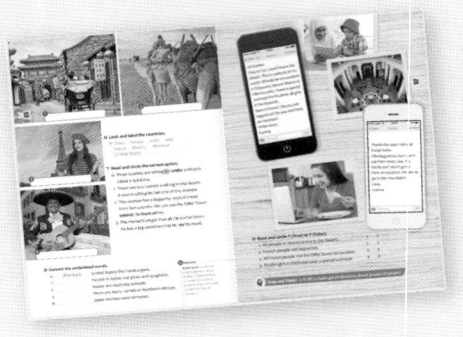

Teaching Tip
Establishing Classroom Guidelines
The first few days of class is a good time to set classroom guidelines. By establishing expectations and routines, you provide students with structure and self-management tools—they know what to expect in terms of both behavior and activities. Before class, decide on three or four guidelines that are important to you, such as: *Respect each other. Listen when others are speaking. Speak in English. Leave food and drinks outside the classroom.* In class, tell students you are going to set the classroom rules together. Elicit ideas and write them on the board. If students don't mention the guidelines you think are important, you might suggest them. As a class, decide on seven or eight guidelines. You can then write them on a poster or turn it into a class project in which everyone helps create the guidelines poster. Once the guidelines poster is ready, you can post it in a visible place in the classroom so you can refer to it when necessary.

Teaching Tip
Guiding Group Discussions
In order to keep students focused and speaking English while they work in small groups, walk around the room and listen to the students' conversations. You may also want to write clear steps on the board showing what exactly you expect students to do, and how long they have to complete each step. Assigning roles to each student in the group, such as note-taker and reporter, can hold students accountable for group work, especially if they come back to a whole-class discussion afterwards.

Objective
Students will be able to use the **verb be, there is, there are**, the **present continuous** and **professions** vocabulary to talk about people, jobs and work-related activities.

Lesson 1   Student's Book p. 8

Warm-up
- Look at the picture at the top of the page.
- Ask students *What kind of food is on the table?*
- Tell students to name as many of the foods they see in the picture as they can.
- Ask *Who are the people? What are they doing?*

1 Look and write *there is* or *there are*.
Students practice using *there is* with singular nouns and *there are* with plural nouns.

Answers
1. There are, 2. There is, 3. there is, 4. There is, 5. there are

2 Label the pictures. What are they advertising?
Students analyze advertisements.
- Ask students to look at the three photos. In pairs, students discuss what each photo shows. (Answer: The first one shows a boy wearing headphones. The second one shows a family on a beach. The third one shows a woman with beautiful hair.)
- Next, tell student pairs to choose which words best describe what each photo is advertising.

Answers
1. music, 2. a beach vacation, 3. shampoo

Extension
Students make connections between photos and other products that could be associated with them.
- Separate students into small groups. Ask *What else can these pictures advertise?*
- Student groups discuss other possible things the photos could advertise.
- After a few minutes, bring the class back together and invite one student in each group to share their answers.

Wrap-up
Students practice *there is* and *there are* in a speaking activity.
- Point to the board and say *There is a board in the classroom.* Then point to some books and say *There are some books in the classroom.*
- Split students up into pairs and tell them to point out the different things around the room and say what they are, using *there is* and *there are*.

(No homework today.)

Teaching Tip
Establishing "Only English" Time
Putting students in pairs and groups for speaking activities can help increase the frequency that they use English in the classroom. However, be sure to monitor students' conversations and make sure they only speak in English. You could put a sign on the board saying "Only English" to show when they should speak English in class. When it is OK to speak other languages, take the sign down.

Unit 0

Lesson 2   Student's Book p. 9

Warm-up

Students brainstorm adjectives they know.
- Split the class into small teams.
- Ask teams to look back at the photo of the family on page eight and think of different adjectives to describe these people (for example, *young, old, happy*).
- Students have three minutes to list as many adjectives as they can. (Use your Stopwatch app to time it.)
- After three minutes, come back together as a whole class. Ask one person from each team to write their adjectives on the board. The team with the most adjectives wins.

3 Answer the questions about the people on page 8.

Students use the verb *be* to answer questions about the people in photos.
- Have students write their answers to the questions.
- After they have answered each question individually, ask students to compare answers in pairs.

Answers

Answers will vary.

4 Write the professions.

Students label photos with the professions they show.

Answers

1. nurse, 2. scientists, 3. truck driver,
4. business people, 5. dancer

5  **Write questions and answers. Then listen and check your answers.**

Students use cues to form questions and write answers to the questions using the photos in Activity 4.

Audio Script

1. What is the nurse doing? He's completing a report.
2. What are the scientists doing? They're working in the lab.
3. What is the truck driver doing? She's talking to her family.
4. What are the business people doing? They're having a meeting.
5. What is the dancer doing? He's dancing ballet.

Stop and Think! Critical Thinking

How does advertising use stereotypes?
- Ask students to think about how advertising uses stereotypes. Point at the photos at the bottom of page 8 and ask *What kinds of stereotypes do you see?*
- Elicit class discussion and guide students to understand that stereotypes are used to appeal to consumers' ideas of how people want to look, feel, act, etc. For example, they may want long, beautiful, shiny hair.

Wrap-up

Students practice the present continuous with professions.
- Split students into teams.
- Give students sentences using the present continuous which describe a profession: *She is giving a patient his medicine. He is having a meeting. She is doing an experiment.*
- The first team to guess which profession each sentence describes gets a point. The team with the most points wins.

➡ **(No homework today.)**

Teaching Tip
Modeling the Activity

Activity instructions can be hard for students to understand, especially for beginners. Use simple wording, and whenever possible, do the first item or two together as a class as a model. Then students can imitate the procedure for the rest of the activity. In this way, you can avoid confusion and misunderstandings and ensure that the activity is effective.

Objective
Students will be able to use the **present simple** as well as **countries**, **nationalities** and **prepositions** vocabulary to talk about people and activities around the world.

Lesson 3 — Student's Book p. 10

Warm-up
Students play a matching game to review countries and nationalities vocabulary.
- Split students into teams.
- Write the names of countries on the board in one column. In another column, write the names of the nationalities that match these countries (scrambled, so that the nationalities are not next to the country they match.) For example:
Countries: *Mexico, France, Italy, Brazil, England*
Nationalities: *Mexican, French, Italian, Brazilian, English*
- Tell teams to match the countries to the correct nationalities. The first team to finish with the correct answers wins.

6 Look and label the countries.
Students write the name of each country below the correct photo.

Answers

1. China, 2. Morocco, 3. France, 4. Mexico

7 Read and circle the correct option.
Students review prepositions of place through descriptions of photos.
- Write the prepositions in the activity on the board: *at, behind, in, in front of, on, under*. Say them aloud and have students repeat.
- Model the meaning of each preposition in the classroom. For example, stand in front of the board and say *I am in front of the board. The board is behind me.*
- Students circle the correct preposition in each sentence.

Answers

1. on, 2. behind, 3. in, on

8 Correct the underlined words.
Students determine what nationality words to use in the sentences.
- Tell students to read the sentence in item 0 and to look at the underlined word and the answer.
- Have students complete the rest of the activity.

Answers

1. Italy, 2. Australian, 3. Africa, 4. Japanese

Extension
Students review the grammar concepts presented in this unit by describing people and places.
- Write *there is* and *there are* on the board. Remind students that we use these to describe people and things in a place. We use *there is* before singular nouns and *there are* before plural nouns.
- Point to the photos on this page. Ask students to describe what they see in each country's photo.
- Elicit a sentence for each photo using *there is* or *there are*. For example, *In Morocco, there are camels.*
- Ask students to describe other countries they know using *there is* and *there are*.

Wrap-up
Students play Hangman to review countries and nationalities.
- Choose a country or nationality word and write a space for each letter in the word on the board. Call on students to guess each letter. Some words to use could be *Morocco, Mexico, China, France, Italy, French, Italian*, etc.

➡ **(No homework today.)**

Unit 0

Lesson 4 Student's Book p. 11

Warm-up

Students look at photos to predict what they are going to read.
- Point to the photos on the page. Ask *What are they doing?* Elicit answers describing actions in the photos.
- Point to the smart phones. Ask students to predict what kind of messages they are going to read: *What are these people going to talk about?*

9 Read and circle T (True) or F (False).

Students read e-mails and answer comprehension questions.

Answers

1. F (Fatima doesn't live in the desert.), 2. T, 3. F (Jeanne doesn't go to Paris on vacation.), 4. T

> **Extension**
> Students write an e-mail.
> - Ask students to imagine that Fatima wrote her e-mail to them. If possible, revise her second paragraph to ask about the students' culture. Project the revised text on the board or hand out printed copies.
> - Ask students to reply to Fatima's e-mail about their country. Use Jeanne's e-mail as a model for this task.

Stop and Think! Critical Thinking

Is it OK to make generalizations about groups of people?
- Ask students *Is it OK to make generalizations about groups of people?*
- Separate students into small groups and ask them to discuss their answers.
- One person in each group should take notes. After five minutes, ask each group to share their ideas. (Use your Stopwatch app to time the discussion.)

Big Question

Students are given the opportunity to reflect on the Big Question.
- Ask students to turn to the unit opener on page 7 and think of some stereotypes they have heard of other nationalities.
- Facilitate discussion of these stereotypes and ask *Are these stereotypes true for all people in these countries?*

➡ **(No homework today.)**

 Teaching Tip

Correcting False Statements

In True / False activities, asking students to correct the false statements helps them to think more critically about the texts they read and confirm their understanding of the text.

1 Why are sports important?

Grammar

Comparative and superlative adjectives: Sports are <u>healthier</u> than video games (comparative).
Jo is the <u>oldest</u> (superlative).

Vocabulary

Sports: baseball, basketball, cricket, cycling, football, rugby, soccer, swimming, tennis, table tennis

Adjectives: active, big, dangerous, expensive, fast, heavy, modern, old, popular, strong, tall

Reading

Knowing when to look up words

Writing

Expressing opinions

Why are sports important?

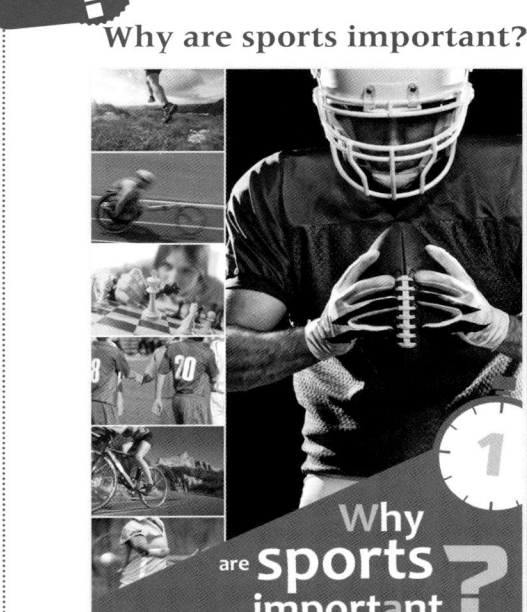

In the first lesson, read the unit title aloud and have students look carefully at the unit cover. Encourage them to think about the message in the picture. At the end of the unit, students will discuss the big question: *Why are sports important?*

Teaching Tip
Personalizing Lessons and Activities
Students will be more engaged in lessons if they feel that they can relate to the content. At the beginning of the school year, try to find out what topics students are interested in and adapt some lessons and activities to the topics they like most.

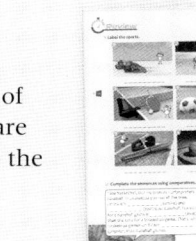
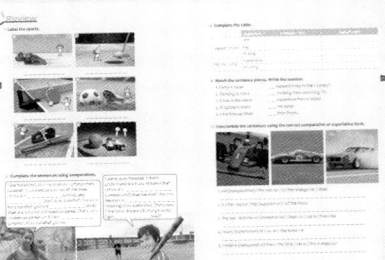

 Vocabulary

Objective
Students will be able to understand and use **sports** vocabulary.

Lesson 1 Student's Book p. 14

Warm-up

Students preview the unit content through group discussion.
- Have students work in small groups.
- Ask students to share three things they each like about sports.
- Ask the groups to vote on the three answers from their groups that they like most.
- As a class, have each group share their three answers. Write the answers on the board.
- Have the class vote on the three answers on the board that they like the most.
- Then ask the class *Why are these things important?* Elicit answers from students.

 16

1 🎧² **Listen and number five sports.**

Students listen to sounds related to different sports and guess which sports they hear.
- Have students write the number of the sound next to the correct sport.

Answers

1. table tennis, 2. soccer, 3. basketball, 4. baseball, 5. tennis

Audio Script

1. [Sounds of ping pong]
2. [Sounds of a soccer game]
3. [Sounds of a basketball game]
4. [Sounds of baseball]
5. [Sounds of tennis: ball bouncing]

2 🎧³ **Listen and write the sports in the map.**

Students listen to the audio and write the names of popular sports next to the correct country on the map.

Answers

Canada: ice hockey, *Cuba*: baseball, *UK and France*: rugby, *China*: table tennis, *India* and *Australia*: cricket

Audio Script

1. Baseball is a modern sport. It's a popular activity in Cuba. There is no time limit in baseball, so you don't need a stopwatch!
2. In Canada the winters are cold. Canadians like to play ice hockey. It's a very fast game.
3. Cricket is a sport played with two teams, a bat and a ball, but the game is older than baseball. Cricket players wear elegant uniforms. Cricket is popular in India and Australia.
4. Rugby looks like a mixture of soccer and American football. It's an exciting sport played in the UK and France. Rugby players don't use any protection, so the sport can be dangerous.
5. The most popular sport of China is table tennis or ping-pong. Table tennis is a fast and active sport.

Wrap-up

Students practice sports names by playing Hangman.
- Use the sports names on page 14.

➡ **Workbook p. 126, Activities 1 and 2**

Lesson 2   Student's Book pp. 14 and 15

✔ **Homework Check!**
Workbook p. 126, Activities 1 and 2
Answers
1 Read and write the name of the sport.
1. swimming, 2. rugby, 3. cycling, 4. soccer,
5. running
2 Unscramble the adjectives.
1. old, 2. big, 3. active, 4. tall, 5. popular

Warm-up
Students review names for sports and choose their favorite ones.
- Write the name of each sport from page 14 on the board. Say them aloud with students.
- Ask students to vote for their favorite sport.
- Say each name and ask students to raise their hands to vote. Each student may only vote once.
- Count the votes and circle the winner. Ask students why they chose the sports they voted for. Elicit a group discussion on these sports' popularity in the class.

3 Classify the words.
Students classify the sports words into three categories: *do* (words that use *do*, e.g., *I do sports*), *play* (words that use *play*, e.g., *I play soccer*), and verbs (e.g., *I swim*).

Answers
Do exercise, judo
Play basketball, tennis
Verb run, swim

4 Think Fast! In your notebook, choose a sport and draw a symbol. A classmate guesses the sport.
Students do a two-minute timed challenge: they review names for sports by drawing symbols for them and guessing the names of the symbols their classmates have drawn.
- Draw students' attention to the **Guess What!** box. Read the information aloud and ask students to guess what sports the other colors represent. Have students look at the map and Activity 2 for clues.

Extension
Ask students which sports from this spread on pages 14 and 15 they have not heard of before or have not played before. Ask *Why do you think you haven't played these sports before? Are they popular here? Why or why not?* Elicit ideas in a group discussion.

Wrap-up
Students review sports words with *do*, *play* and verbs by completing sentences on the board.
- Write the following phrases on the board with gaps for students to fill: *We ____ basketball. / I ____ yoga. / Richard ____.*
- Students should choose from the following words to complete the phrases: *swims, do, play*.
- Elicit answers from the class. The first student to answer all three correctly wins.

 **Workbook pp. 126 and 127, Activities 3 – 5**

💭 Teaching Tip
Respecting Differences
It is important for students to know that it is a good thing that they have different likes and dislikes from each other. By respecting each other's differences, they can learn from each other and gain new insights.

Grammar

Objectives
Students will be able to use **comparatives** and **superlatives** to talk about sports.

Lesson 3 — Student's Book p. 16

> ✔ Homework Check!
> Workbook pp. 126 and 127, Activities 3–5
> **Answers**
> **3 Write sentences using the adjectives.**
> Answers will vary.
> **4 Label the pictures.**
> 1. strong, 2. elegant, 3. heavy, 4. fast,
> 5. complicated
> **5 Match.**
> *2nd* second, *3rd* third, *4th* fourth, *5th* fifth

Warm-up

Students compare sports by choosing activities they like.

- Write the following sentences on the board in pairs: *He swims. – She runs. / We play soccer. – They play baseball. / I do judo. – She does exercise.*

- Have students work in groups to choose the activities they like most out of each pair.

- Have groups present their choices to the class. Ask students why they chose their answers. Keep count on the board of how many groups chose each activity to see which activities won the most "likes."

1 Match the sentence pieces.
Students preview the comparative by matching sentence pieces.
- Check answers as a class. Tell students to pay special attention to the words in bold. Ask *What do the bold words mean?*

Answers
1. Soccer is more popular than swimming. 2. The time for a soccer game is longer than a basketball game. 3. Mark swims faster than Peter. 4. The rules for soccer are more complicated than for swimming. 5. A soccer outfit is more expensive than a swimming outfit. 6. A soccer field is bigger than a swimming pool. 7. Soccer and swimming are healthier than video games!

2 In your notebook, write the comparative forms.
Students practice using comparative forms with the words provided.
- Draw students' attention to the **Comparatives** box at the bottom of the page. Read the content aloud and point out how we form comparatives for words with one syllable or two syllables ending in *-y* (by adding *–er* and *than*) and for words with two or more syllables (by adding *more* and *than*).

Answers
faster, older, healthier, more expensive, more active, more elegant

Wrap-up

Students review comparatives.
- Write the following words on the board: *young, small, intelligent*.
- Have students guess the comparative form for each word. Then ask the student who answers for each adjetive to use the comparative form in a sentence. (Answers: younger, smaller, more intelligent)

➡ **Workbook p. 127, Activities 1 and 2**

Lesson 4
Student's Book p. 17

> ✔ **Homework Check!**
> Workbook p. 127, Activities 1 and 2
> **Answers**
> **1 Complete the sentences about you and your friends or family.**
> Answers will vary.
> **2 Look and write comparisons.**
> 1. Bike B is faster than Bike A.
> 2. Bike A is more original than Bike B.
> 3. Bike A is bigger than Bike B.
> 4. Bike B is more modern than Bike A.
> 5. Bike A is taller than Bike B.
> 6. Bike B is more popular than Bike A.

Warm-up
Students review comparative forms by completing sentences.
- Write the following phrases on the board with gaps for students to fill: 1. *I am ____ (fast) Tim.* / 2. *Lisa is ____ (old) Rachel.* / 3. *Tom is ____ (active) James.*
- Have students independently complete the sentences with the correct comparative form and check answers as a class.

Answers
1. faster than, 2. older than, 3. more active than

3 Study the table and write *volleyball*, *basketball* or *tennis*.
Students are exposed to superlative forms by completing sentences.
- Tell students to pay special attention to the words in bold. Ask *What do the bold words mean?*

Answers
1. Volleyball, 2. basketball, 3. tennis, 4. basketball

4 Label the pictures with the superlative form.
Students practice writing superlative forms.
- Draw students' attention to the **Superlatives** box at the bottom of the page. Read the information aloud. Point out how we form superlatives for words with one syllable or two syllables ending in -y (by adding *the* and *–est*) and for words with two or more syllables (by adding *the most*).

Answers
1. the tallest, 2. the strongest, 3. the most expensive, 4. the oldest

5 Think Fast! In your notebook, write five adjectives in their three forms: regular, comparative and superlative.
Students do a three-minute timed challenge: they practice writing adjectives in regular, comparative and superlative forms.

> **Extension**
> Have students turn back to pages 14 and 15 and look at the map. Ask students to tell you which sports are the most popular in each country on the map. Go over the answers as a class.

Wrap-up
Students review the superlative form by completing sentences.
- Write the following phrases on the board with gaps for students to fill: 1. *I am ____ (fast) on the team.* / 2. *Lisa is ____ (old) in the group.* / 3. *Tom is ____ (active) student in his class.*
- Have students independently complete the sentences with the correct superlative form and check answers as a class.

Answers
1. the fastest, 2. the oldest, 3. the most active

➡ **Workbook p. 128, Activities 3 and 4**

Reading & Writing

Objectives
Students will be able determine the meaning of words from the context. They will also be able to express their opinions.

Lesson 5 Student's Book pp. 18 and 19

✔ **Homework Check!**
Workbook p. 128, Activities 3 and 4

Answers
3 Find the adjectives. Circle with gray or blue.

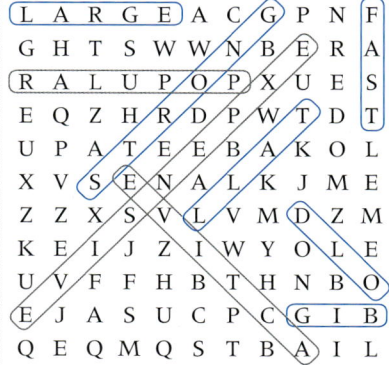

2 Correct the sentences.
1. ~~older~~ My grandpa is the oldest.
2. ~~happier~~ My dad is the happiest person in this picture.
3. ~~nicer~~ I have the nicest hair!
4. ~~big~~ My dad has the biggest muscles.
5. ~~shorter~~ I am the shortest of the three.

Warm-up
Students preview the article and have a class discussion.
- Ask students to preview the article by looking at the title and the pictures on pages 18 and 19.
- Have students discuss in pairs what they think the people are doing. Make sure students do not begin reading the article.
- After a few minutes, bring the class together to share ideas. Ask if the class agrees or disagrees, and why or why not.

1 Look at the pictures and read the title. Then circle *Yes* or *No*.
Students preview the article and circle *Yes* or *No* for each question.

Answers
1. No, 2. No, 3. No

2 Read the article. Then use red or green to circle the underlined words.
Students read the article and indicate whether or not they understood words from context.
- Draw students' attention to the **Be Strategic!** box and read the information aloud. After students have completed the activity, ask them which of the words they circled in red they think they should look up in a dictionary.
- Compare answers and ask students why it seems important to look up a particular word or not.

Wrap-up
Students discuss parkour as a class.
- Ask students *Is parkour popular here? Why or why not?*
- Have students discuss the question as a class.

▶ **Workbook p. 129, Activities 1 – 3**

🎵 **Teaching Tip**
Managing Fast Finishers
Some students complete activities more quickly than others so it's a good idea to have a few extra activities on hand, otherwise these students may become bored and disruptive. One set of activities designed for fast finishers are the *Just for Fun* pages. Students can work on these individually and then check their answers in the back of the Student's Book. The *Just for Fun* activities for this unit are on page 26.

Lesson 6 — Student's Book pp. 18 and 19

✔ **Homework Check!**
Workbook p. 129, Activities 1 – 3

Answers
1 Read the article and label the pictures.
left to right Joshua, Leon
2 Use red or green to circle the underlined words in the article.
Answers will vary.
3 Label the picture.
clockwise from left skateboarder, protection, skateboard

Warm-up
Students review the underlined words from the article.
- Write each underlined word from the article on page 18 on the board.
- Ask students to give a definition of each word. Write the definitions on the board and ask the class if they agree or disagree with the given definition. Students may correct their classmates if the definition is not correct.
- Ask students which clues they used from context to come up with their definitions.

3 Complete the dictionary entries with two of the underlined words.
Students complete dictionary entries with words from the article.

Answers
train, *train*, traceur, *traceur*

4 Read the notes and write complete paragraphs.
Students read the notes and write complete paragraphs describing people's opinions on parkour.

> **Extension**
> Ask students for their own opinions on parkour. Split students into small groups to discuss whether they think parkour is a cool sport or if it is too dangerous. Circulate around the room and listen in on students' conversations. After five minutes, ask students to summarize their groups' opinions for the class.

Stop and Think! Critical Thinking
Is it OK to participate in a dangerous sport?
- Ask students the question and elicit answers. Encourage students to give reasons for their answers: *Why is it OK or why is it not OK?*

Wrap-up
Students discuss dangerous sports as a class.
- Ask students to think of other examples of dangerous sports. Elicit ideas from students and ask them what makes these sports dangerous. Ask if it is OK to participate in these sports and why. Do students agree?

⮕ **Workbook p. 129, Activities 4 and 5**

Preparing for the Next Lesson
Ask students to watch an introduction to cycling in Holland: https://youtu.be/SfLJ876lXsQ or invite them to look around on the blog about cycling in The Netherlands: goo.gl/UOoym1.

> 🐝 **Teaching Tip**
> **Talking about Opinions**
> Teenagers may have strong opinions on subjects like sports and popular culture. Remind students that it is OK to agree or disagree and to be respectful of each other's opinions. If a discussion about one sport gets too tense, try changing the subject to another sport that might produce less tension.

# Culture

Objective
Students will be able to use **comparatives** to talk about the environmental advantages of green transportation.

Lesson 7   Student's Book p. 20

> ✔ **Homework Check!**
> Workbook p. 129, Activities 4 and 5
>
> **Answers**
> **4 Write two of the underlined words that correspond.**
> trick, *tricks*; adult, *adult*
> **5 Follow the instructions.**
> Answers will vary.

Warm-up
Students brainstorm comparisons of bikes and cars using comparatives.
- Write the following adjectives on the board: *fast, convenient, healthy, comfortable*.
- Ask students to create sentences comparing bikes and cars using these adjectives. Students should use the comparative form.
- Ask student volunteers to write their sentences on the board. Check answers as a class.

1 Look at the pictures and discuss the questions.
Students preview the rap by looking at the pictures and discussing the questions.

Answers
1. Answers will vary; example: people of all ages,
2. No, 3. Answers will vary; example: transportation

2 🎧⁴ Listen to the rap and read along.
Students listen to the rap and read along with the audio.

Audio Script
Bikes in Holland
I watch a program on TV
Bikes are a fascination
In Holland, as you can see
It is their transportation

There are bikes in the rain
And bicycles in the snow
Those bikes are everywhere you go!

A father cycling with his kids
A grandmother alone
The whole country is—I think:
A giant biking zone!

Businessmen ride bikes
And businesswomen, too
I want to ride one; how about you?

---

3 Number the pictures.
Students number the pictures based on their descriptions in the rap.

Answers
left to right, top to bottom 5, 2, 1, 3, 4

Wrap-up
Ask students when else people might use bikes. Elicit ideas from students. For example, people might ride bikes for sports (like in races), or for exercise in a gym (on an exercise bike) or in a park.

▶ **(No homework today.)**

Lesson 8
Student's Book p. 21

Warm-up
Students review the rap from page 20 again.
- Play the rap from page 20 again and have students read along.

4 Answer the questions.
Students answer the questions in groups.
- Separate students into small groups. Ask students to discuss the questions together. Each group should have one "recorder" (someone who takes notes) to take notes on their answers. Each group should also have one "presenter" (someone who presents the group's answers to the class).
- As students discuss, circulate around the room and listen to students' conversations.
- After 10 minutes, bring the class together. Have the presenter from each group explain their group's answers. Ask the class if they agree or disagree with each group and why.

Stop and Think! Critical Thinking
Is your city bicycle friendly?
- Ask the same student groups to discuss this question. Groups should have new recorders and presenters this time. After about five minutes, bring the class back together. Ask presenters to present their ideas. Ask the class if they agree or disagree with each group and why.

Wrap-up
Students use the comparative to describe Holland's and their city's bike use.
- Write the following sentence on the board with gaps for students to fill: *Holland / My city is _____ (bike friendly) than Holland / my city.*
- Ask students to choose *Holland* or *My city* at the beginning and end of the sentence and to use the comparative form of *bike friendly*.
- Continue with other sentences like *Cycling in the rain is _____ (easy) than cycling in the snow. / Riding a bike to school is _____ (healthy) than going in a car.*

➡ **(No homework today.)**

 **Project**

> **Objective**
> Students will be able to use **sports** vocabulary to create a sports manual.

Lesson 9   Student's Book pp. 22 and 23

Warm-up

Students describe a game they know well.
- Tell students to work in pairs.
- Have pairs choose a game they know well. This can be a board game or a card game.
- Have students write notes on how to play the game and where it is popular.
- After 10 minutes, ask student pairs to present their games to the class.

 24

1 Make a sports manual.
Students create a sports manual for their favorite sport.
- Have students work in pairs to create their sports manual.
- Have students follow the instructions on pages 22 and 23. Circulate around the room to help as needed.
- Inform students that they will present their manuals in class the next day.

> **The Digital Touch**
> To incorporate digital media in the project, suggest one or more of the following:
> - Students can write and design their manuals using Word or PowerPoint, or with a program like Google Docs or Slides.
> - Students can find photos on the Internet or can take photos with a smart phone to illustrate their manuals.
>
> Note that students should have the option to do a task on paper or digitally.

Wrap-up

Have two pairs of students work together to give each other feedback on their manuals.
- Have students compare their manuals and get feedback. Ask students to make sure their manuals are clear and make sense. They will present their manuals in the next class.

 **Teaching Tip**
Giving Peer Feedback
Students can offer valuable feedback to each other. Ask students to review each other's projects to make sure the information is clear.

Lesson 10 Student's Book pp. 22 and 23

Warm-up
- Have students review their sports manuals to prepare for their presentations. Give them about 10 minutes to review their information before beginning.

Extension
Students present their sports manuals in small groups. Students should present their manuals to their groups, describing all the information clearly and showing illustrations. Circulate around the room and listen to students' presentations. After each pair of student finishes, the other students in the group can ask questions. Make sure students present to their group and have a chance to answer questions.

Wrap-up
Students use comparative and superlative adjectives to describe the sports their classmates presented.
- In the same groups, have students write sentences describing the different sports they heard about. Students should write five sentences using at least one superlative and three comparative forms.
- Groups present their sentences and are awarded one point for each unique comparative or superlative (one that was not used by another group). The group with the most points wins.

 **Workbook p. 128, Activity 1 (Review)**

Teaching Tip
Planning Presentations
For small group presentations, you can decide how much time each presentation should take, and how much time students have to ask and answer questions before moving on to the next presentation. This depends on how long your class is and how many students you have in a class.

Review

Objectives
Students will be able to use **comparatives** and **superlatives** to talk about sports.

Lesson 11   Student's Book p. 24

> ✔ **Homework Check!**
> Workbook p. 128, Activity 1 (Review)
> **Answers**
> **1 Complete about you!**
> Answers will vary.

 Warm-up
Students review comparatives on the board.
- Write the following adjectives on the board: *small, young, active, intelligent, fast*.
- Have students volunteer to write the comparative form of each word on the board. Ask the class if they agree or disagree.
- Elicit example sentences from the class using each comparative form.

1 Label the sports.
Students review sports vocabulary by labeling pictures.

Answers
1. swimming, 2. golf, 3. table tennis, 4. soccer, 5. baseball, 6. basketball

2 Complete the sentences using comparatives.
Students complete sentences with the comparative forms of adjectives given as cues.

Answers
more active, faster, longer, more popular
more complicated, more relaxing, older

> **Extension**
> - Ask students to compare two sports on their own, using the paragraphs in Activity 2 as a model. Students should use at least four comparatives in their paragraphs. After they are done writing, have students exchange their paragraphs with a partner to check their comparatives. If there is time, ask for volunteers to share their paragraphs with the class.

Wrap-up
Students review words for sports by playing Hangman.
- Use different sports words from this unit, starting with Lesson 1. Ask students if the sports are popular in their country.

▶ **(No homework today.)**

Lesson 12 Student's Book p. 25

Warm-up
Students review superlatives on the board.
- Write the following adjectives on the board: *small, young, active, intelligent, fast*.
- Have students volunteer to write the superlative form of each word on the board. Ask the class if they agree or disagree.
- Elicit example sentences from the class using each superlative form.

3 Complete the table.
Students complete the table with the comparative and superlative forms of the adjectives given.

Answers
old older, oldest; *big* bigger, biggest; *strong* stronger, strongest; *expensive* more expensive, most expensive; *exciting* more exciting, most exciting

4 Match the sentence pieces. Write the number.
Students review comparatives and superlatives by matching the beginnings of the sentences with their correct endings.

Answers
top to bottom 3, 2, 4, 5, 1

5 Unscramble the sentences using the correct comparative or superlative form.
Students practice using comparative and superlative forms by writing complete sentences using cues.

Answers
1. The red car is older than the orange car.
2. The red car is the biggest of the three.
3. The red car is more expensive than the blue car.
4. Car #1 is the heaviest of the three.
5. The blue car is more modern than the orange car.

? Big Question
Students are given the opportunity to revisit the Big Question and reflect on it.
- Ask students to turn to the unit cover on page 13.
- Ask them to name the sports. (From top to bottom: running, wheelchair racing, chess, soccer, cycling and tennis. In the large picture: football).
- Elicit how the sports in the pictures are different. (One athlete is in a wheelchair. Chess is not a physical sport. Soccer is the only team sport.)
- Remind students of the texts in the unit: *Do you think parkour is a sport? Do you think cycling to school could be considered a sport? So what is a sport?*
- Most importantly, ask students to relate sports to their own lives: *What physical activities do you do regularly? Do you play sports, even if it isn't team sports? Would you like to play a new sport?*

★ Scorecard
Hand out (and/or project) a *Scorecard*. Have students fill in their *Scorecards* for this unit.

▶ **Study for the unit test.**

2 How do you get around?

Grammar

Imperatives: <u>Turn</u> left. <u>Don't park</u> here.

Irregular comparative and superlative adjectives: This park is <u>better</u> than the one downtown, but the one by my house is the <u>best</u>.

Vocabulary

Places in a City: bank, coffee shop, convenience store, drugstore, mall, park, school, supermarket

Transportation: bike, bus, car, motorcycle, plane, subway, train

Listening

Following directions on a map

Reading

Identifying the objective of a text

How do you get around?

In the first lesson, read the unit title aloud and have students look carefully at the unit cover. Encourage them to think about the message in the picture. At the end of the unit, students will discuss the big question: *How do you get around?*

Teaching Tip

Teaching about Other Cultures

In the unit cover, students will notice that the photo may show a different culture than their own. It is important to let students know that even though the cultures are different, they have a lot of similarities. This will help them to open their minds about different cultures and people.

 **Vocabulary**

Objective
Students will be able to use **places in a city** and **transportation** vocabulary.

Lesson 1   Student's Book pp. 28 and 29

Warm-up
Students discuss the ways they come to school and go home every day.
- Ask students *How do you come to school?* Elicit answers from students. Write their answers on the board.
- Ask students *Do you all come to school the same way? What is different?*
- Ask *How do you go home? Is it the same way?* Elicit answers to facilitate discussion.

1 🎧⁵ **Listen and number the places on the map.**
Students preview vocabulary for places in a city by listening to audio and labeling the map.

Answers

park 1, *mall* 8, *drugstore* 4, *coffee shop* 3, *convenience store* 7, *bank* 5, *school* 6, *supermarket* 2

Audio Script

Hi, and welcome to Chronopolis! My name's Emma and I'm going to show you some places in the city.
1. There is a nice little park on Green Street. I like to sit in the park.
2. There is a supermarket downtown. You can buy a lot of things at the supermarket.
3. I have a favorite coffee shop. Its name is Awesome Coffee Shop.
4. The biggest drugstore is on Willow Avenue. You can buy medicine there night and day.
5. My mom works at a bank. It's called ChronoBank.
6. My favorite place in town: my school. I love studying.
7. There is a convenience store on Black Street. It's like a small supermarket.
8. We have a mall in our city, too. The mall is my friends' favorite place.

2 Read and mark (✓) the correct places.
Students continue practicing vocabulary for places in a city by identifying the places where they do certain activities.

Answers

1. drugstore, 2. bank, 3. coffee shop, 4. mall, 5. convenience store

Wrap-up
Students play Charades to review places in a city vocabulary.
- Write the places in a city vocabulary on slips of paper, copying each vocabulary item onto two slips. Fold the slips so the word is not visible and put each set in a separate box or bowl.
- Divide the class into teams. Have one student from each team volunteer to act out a vocabulary word at a time.
- Teams take turns. The actor from one team picks a slip. The student acts out the vocabulary word and his or her team tries to guess the place in a city. Use the Stopwatch app to time the team, giving them one or two minutes to guess each word. Each correct guess is worth one point.
- The team with the most points wins.

➡ **Workbook p. 130, Activity 1**

 **Teaching Tip**

Keeping a Vocabulary Notebook
Encourage students to write new vocabulary in their vocabulary notebook. Even though the words are written in their Student's Book, they can keep all their new vocabulary in one place in their notebooks. This makes it easy for them to review quickly.

Lesson 2 Student's Book pp. 28 and 29

> ✔ **Homework Check!**
> Workbook p. 130, Activity 1
> Answers
> **1 Label the places on the map.**
> 1. supermarket, 2. mall, 3. park, 4. drugstore, 5. bank

Warm-up
Students review vocabulary for places around town.
- Have students close their books. Ask students questions to review vocabulary for places around town. For example:
  - *Where do you buy medicine?* (Drugstore)
  - *Where do you put money?* (Bank)
  - *Where do you learn?* (School)
  - *Where do people go for a hot drink?* (Coffee shop)
  - *Where do people buy lots of clothes?* (Mall)
  - *You want a hot sandwich. Where do you go?* (Convenience store)
  - *Your family needs food. Where do you go?* (Supermarket)
  - *Where can you play outside?* (Park)

3 Classify the forms of transportation in the chart.
Students practice using transportation vocabulary by classifying words.
- Tell students that *public* means we share it, and *private* means we use it by ourselves.
- Draw students' attention to the **Guess What!** box. Tell them that "bike" and "plane" are other ways of saying "bicycle" and "airplane."

Answers
Public bus, plane, subway, train
Private bicycle, car, motorcycle

4 Think Fast! Count all the bikes, buses and motorcycles on the map.
Students do a two-minute timed challenge: they identify and count all of the bikes, buses and motorcycles on the map.
- Have students race to count the items. Have students raise their hands when they are done.
- Check students' answers. The first student to count them all wins.

Answers
bikes 6, *buses* 3, *motorcycles* 3

5 Listen and circle the correct option.
Students practice transportation vocabulary and listening comprehension.

Answers
1. bike, 2. train, 3. plane, 4. car

Audio Script
1. Alyssa
   BOY: Watch out!
2. Ben
   ANNOUNCER OVER A PA SYSTEM: The next train to arrive at Platform 3 is the 12:15 train to Chronopolis.
3. Cathy
   FLIGHT ATTENDANT: Ladies and gentlemen, welcome aboard Time Airways flight 998 with service from Chronopolis to London. We ask you to please keep your seatbelt fastened and keep all luggage underneath your seat.
4. Dan
   BOY: Mom! I'm late for school!
   WOMAN: Don't worry, honey! We'll make it on time.

Wrap-up
Students race to identify transportation vocabulary.
- Divide the class into teams of seven (maximum).
- Explain that each team will send one student to the board at a time, and you will give them a hint about a form of transportation. The students at the board race to write the correct transportation vocabulary word.
- The student who writes the correct word fastest (including correct spelling) wins a point for his or her team.
- You can use hints like these: *I have two wheels and an engine.* (Motorcycle).; *I have pedals.* (Bike); *I fly.* (Plane); *I move on rails all across the country.* (Train); *I drive on the streets and carry lots of passengers.* (Bus); *I go underground.* (Subway); *I carry two to five people.* (Car).

▶ **Workbook pp. 130 and 131, Activities 2–4**

Grammar

Objective
Students will learn to use the **imperatives** to give directions.

Lesson 3   Student's Book p. 30

> ✔ **Homework Check!**
> Workbook pp. 130 and 131, Activities 2–4
>
> **Answers**
> **2 Label the pictures and cross out the letters you use.**
> a̶a̶a̶a̶ b̶b̶b̶ c̶c̶c̶ e̶e̶e̶e̶ f i̶i̶i̶ k l̶l̶ m n̶n̶ o̶o̶ p r̶r̶r̶r̶ s̶s̶ t̶t̶t̶ u̶u̶u̶ w̶ y̶y̶y̶
> 1. bike, 2. train, 3. plane, 4. car, 5. subway, 6. motorcycle
> **3 Unscramble the remaining letters to label the picture.**
> e f r r y: ferry
> **4 Circle the correct options.**
> 1. ride a motorcycle, 2. ride in a car, 3. ride a bike, 4. plane, 5. ride a motorcycle

Warm-up
Students preview how to give directions.
Have students look at the map on pages 30 and 31.
- Ask *What does the map show?* Elicit answers from students. (Answer: The map shows a neighborhood in London.)
- Ask *What do the dotted lines show?* (Answer: The lines show how someone gets from Waterloo station to Westminster Abbey.)

1 Read and follow the directions on the map.
Students practice following written directions by tracing a route on the map.

2 Read the directions again and number the arrows.
Students continue practicing how to give and follow directions by matching icons to written directions.
- Draw students' attention to the **Imperatives** box on page 30 and read the information aloud. Explain that imperatives give commands. We use imperatives to give directions or instructions and to tell people to do things.
- Students write the number of the directions next to the matching arrows.

Answers
left to right, top to bottom 2, 4, 1, 5, 3

Extension
Students practice giving directions in a class discussion.
- Ask students how to get to a place near their classroom. This could be the school library, the cafeteria, or another classroom they know well.
- If needed, draw a map from the classroom to the place on the board. Draw lines and arrows following students' directions.

Wrap-up
Students review giving directions.
- Ask students to give directions from their desks to different parts of the classroom, like the board, the teacher's desk, the door, etc.
- Have one student volunteer to give directions. Ask for another volunteer to follow the directions. Repeat with different locations in the room and different volunteers.

➡ **Workbook p. 131, Activities 1 and 2**

 Teaching Tip
Previewing Grammar and Vocabulary
When previewing new grammar or vocabulary, it is OK for students to make mistakes. This is a time to *preview* the language and experiment with it before they completely learn it.

Lesson 4
Student's Book p. 31

> ✔ **Homework Check!**
> Workbook p. 131, Activities 1 and 2
> **Answers**
> **1 Unscramble the letters to complete the directions.**
> 1. Don't go, 2. Turn, 3. Cross, 4. right
> **2 Correct the directions to match the route on the map.**
> 1. Go past the mall.
> 2. Turn right on Milford Avenue.
> 3. Turn right into Triple Oak Park and cross through it.
> 4. Oak Coffee Shop is on the left.

Warm-up
Students practice giving directions using the London map on pages 30 and 31.
- Ask students to look at the map. Say *I'm at Victoria Embankment and I need to go to the Aquarium. Do I turn right on Bridge Street?*
- Elicit answers from students. (Answer: No, turn left on Bridge Street.)
- Repeat with other locations on the map.

3 Look at the signs. Correct the sentences.
Students correct the sentences to match the signs.

Answers
1. Stop here.
2. Don't park your car here.
3. Turn left.
4. Don't drive over 50 km/h.
5. Don't turn right.
6. Don't ride your bike here.

4 Think Fast! In your notebook, write directions from the London Eye to Westminster Abbey.
Students do a two-minute timed challenge: they practice writing directions from the London Eye to Westminster Abbey.

Answers
1. When you leave the London Eye, turn left on The Queen's Walk. Walk straight ahead.
2. Go past the Sea Life London Aquarium.
3. Turn right and cross Westminster Bridge. Go past Big Ben.
4. Turn left on Parliament Street, and then take the first right.
5. Turn left at Saint Margaret's Church and walk straight ahead.

5 Listen to some tourists at Waterloo Station. Mark (✓) the correct options.
Students practice using irregular comparatives and superlatives with a listening activity.
- Draw students' attention to the *Comparatives and Superlatives–Irregular Forms* box and read the information aloud.

Answers
1. the best, 2. farther, 3. the worst

Audio Script
1. GIRL: I think the London Eye is the best tourist attraction in London.
   BOY: Really? I don't know… I love the British Museum. Their Egyptian collection is amazing.
2. MAN: Look, according to the map, Big Ben is farther than the London Eye.
   WOMAN: Hmm… let me look at it. Yes, that's right, Big Ben is farther. Let's go to the London Eye first.
   MAN: Great!
3. WOMAN: Bus or subway… Which should we take to visit the attractions?
   MAN: I think we should get a car. Let's rent one over there…
   WOMAN: No way! Cars are the worst option! Taking the subway or a bus is a better means of transportation for tourists in London.

Stop and Think! Critical Thinking
In your opinion, what are the best and the worst places in your city?
- Students work in pairs or in small groups to discuss the question.
- After five minutes, ask groups to share their answers. (Use your Stopwatch app to time it.) Ask if students in each group agreed or disagreed and why.

Wrap-up
Students review irregular comparatives and superlatives in a group discussion.
- Write the following sentences on the board with gaps for students to fill: ____ is better than ____. / ____ is the best. / ____ is worse than ____. / ____ is the worst.
- Students complete the sentences with different places in town and share their answers with the class.

➡ **Workbook p. 132, Activity 3**

Listening & Reading

Objectives
Students will be able to follow directions on a map. They will also be able to identify the objective of a text.

Lesson 5 — Student's Book p. 32

> ✔ **Homework Check!**
> Workbook p. 132, Activity 3
> **Answers**
> **3 Circle the correct words to complete the opinions.**
> 1. the best; 2. far, farther than; 3. the worst; 4. bad, worse than

Warm-up
Students play a game in small groups.
- Write places in the classroom on slips of paper: *the door, the board, the teacher's desk*, etc., and place them face down on a desk or table.
- Separate students into small groups. Each group should be in a different corner of the classroom.
- Have each group choose one student to follow the group's directions (the walker).
- Students pick a slip of paper and compete to give their walker directions to get their destination fastest.

1 🎧⁸ **Listen to the directions and follow the route on the map. Write the places below.**
Students follow directions given in an audio and follow the route on the map.
- Draw students' attention to the **Be Strategic!** box and read the information aloud. Ask students to find the label "You are here" on the map. This is where they should begin.

Answers
Destination 1 8-12 Convenience Store
Destination 2 Awesome Coffee

Audio Script
1. We're ready. Let's go.
   Walk straight ahead on Oak Street. Turn right on Black Street. Walk straight ahead. Cross Willow Avenue and Pine Street. Your destination is on the left, between Pine and Maple.
2. We're ready. Let's go.
   Walk straight ahead on Black Street. Cross Pine Street and Willow Avenue. Go past the bank. Turn right on Oak Street. Walk straight ahead. Cross Purple street. Your destination is on the right.

2 Complete the instructions and write the destination. Start at the entrance of Green Park.
Students continue to practice giving directions by completing the instructions.

Answers
Walk, Turn, Chrono Bank

3 Work with a partner. Give directions to a place on the map. Start at the X-Mall.
Students practice giving and listening to directions.
- Draw students' attention to the **Guess What!** box. Read the information aloud. Students should understand that we usually abbreviate Street as St. and Avenue as Ave.

Wrap-up
Students review vocabulary for places in a city by talking about places they went.
- Separate students into pairs.
- Ask students to tell their partners about places in town they have been to: *I went to the drugstore to get medicine.*
- Tell students to share their sentences with the class.

▶ **Workbook p. 133, Activities 1 and 2**

> 💭 **Teaching Tip**
> **Managing Fast Finishers**
> Some students complete activities more quickly than others, so it's a good idea to have a few extra activities on hand, otherwise these students may become bored and disruptive. One set of activities designed for fast finishers are the *Just for Fun* pages. Students can work on these individually and then check their answers in the back of the Student's Book. The *Just for Fun* activities for this unit are on page 40.

Lesson 6
Student's Book p. 33

✔ **Homework Check!**
Workbook p. 133, Activities 1 and 2

Answers
1 Look at the text below. Mark (✓) the correct option.
2. It's an interview.
2 Complete the text with the questions below.
1. worst place in town, 2. why is it the worst place, 3. do you like the X-Mall, 4. your favorite store

Warm-up
Students have a group discussion about signs in town.
- Ask students where they usually see signs in town. Ask *Are they all for traffic? What purposes do they have?* Elicit student answers and discuss as a class.

4 Look at the text below and mark (✓) its objective.
Students read the text quickly and identify its purpose.

Answers
to give information about signs

5 Read the text again. Write the places in Chronopolis where the signs are located.
Students make inferences from the text and relate the information to a map.
- Tell students to label where each sign is in Chronopolis.
- Remind students that they can refer to the map in Activity 1.

Answers
Sign 1 X-Mall, *Sign 2* Awesome Coffee, *Sign 3* Green Park

6 Circle T (True) or F (False).
Students identify whether statements about the text are true or false.

Answers
1. F (All the pictures are from Chronopolis.), 2. T, 3. F (The billboard is huge.), 4. F (*Keep calm...* signs are very popular.), 5. T

Extension
Students make a sign for their town.
- Form small groups and ask groups to create a sign for their town.
- They may draw it on a piece of paper, on the board or make it using a computer.
- Ask students to discuss the following questions about their signs: *What is it for? Where does it go? Who reads it?*
- Ask each group to present their sign to the class.

Wrap-up
Students discuss signs used in school.
- Ask students *What do we use signs for in school?* Elicit answers from students.
- If you have any signs in the classroom, ask students *Why do we have this sign?* and *Do we need any other signs?*

▶ **Workbook p. 133, Activity 3**

Preparing for the Next Lesson
Ask students to watch an introduction to the London Underground: goo.gl/pJnzEv or invite them to look around on the Transport for London web site: tfl.gov.uk.

Culture

Objective
Students will be able to use **imperatives** and **transportation** vocabulary to talk about getting around London.

Lesson 7   Student's Book p. 34

> ✔ **Homework Check!**
> Workbook p. 133, Activity 3
> **Answers**
> 3 Look at the map in Activity 2 on page 32. In your notebook, write directions to two places.
> Answers will vary.

Warm-up
Students preview the topic of the lesson by discussing the pictures on pages 34 and 35.
- Ask students to look at the pictures on pages 34 and 35. Ask *What city do you see?* and *What form of transportation do you see on page 35? What do you think is special about it?* Elicit answers from students.

1 🎧⁹ **Look at the map. Listen and answer the questions.**
Students learn about the London Underground by looking at the map while listening to the audio. Note that the Underground is the *subway* in London.

Answers
1. yellow and green, 2. District, 3. red, brown and light blue

Audio Script
GUIDE: Okay. Is everybody here? What is the name of this Underground station?
BOY: Blackfriars.
GUIDE: Right! This is Blackfriars Station. Now, look at your maps and find Blackfriars Station. Got it? Blackfriars is on two Underground lines. What colors are the lines on the map?
NARRATOR: Answer, question 1.
GIRL: I know! One is yellow and the other is green.
GUIDE: That's right. The Circle Line is the yellow line on the map. Now, what is the name of the green line?
NARRATOR: Answer, question 2.
GIRL: The green line is the District Line.
GUIDE: Great! Now, we will be traveling to the Tower of London. It's at Oxford Circus Station. Oxford Circus is on three Underground lines. What colors are the Underground lines at Oxford Circus Station?
NARRATOR: Answer, question 3.
BOY: That's easy. They're red and brown and light blue.

2 Plan your trip to Oxford Circus.
Students use the map to plan a trip to Oxford Circus on the London Underground.
- Tell students to look at the map on page 35 and plan a trip to Oxford Circus. Students should start from the Blackfriars station on the right side of the map.

Answers
yellow/Circle or green/District, Embankment, brown/Bakerloo, Oxford Circus

> **Extension**
> Students use the map to plan more trips.
> - Ask students to plan a trip from Oxford Circus station to other stations, like Hyde Park Corner, High Street Kensington or Victoria.

Wrap-up
Students discuss the places they would like to visit in London.
- Ask students if there are any places they would like to visit in London. Some examples could be Big Ben, Buckingham Palace or Hyde Park.
- Ask students how they could get to these places on the London Underground from Blackfriars station. Elicit answers. (Note: Big Ben is at Westminster station; Buckingham Palace is at Green Park station; Hyde Park is at Lancaster Gate station.)

➡ **(No homework today.)**

> **Teaching Tip**
> **Preparing for a Listening Activity**
> Ask students to preview questions before they listen to audio or read an article. This will help guide their reading and listening for the information they need to find.

Lesson 8
Student's Book pp. 34 and 35

Warm-up
Students review language for giving directions together on the board.
- Have students close their books.
- Draw arrows on the board, similar to the ones on page 30, Activity 2.
- Ask students to tell what each arrow means. Elicit answers from students.

3 Think Fast! Plan a trip from Blackfriars Station to Hyde Park Corner.
Students do a two-minute timed challenge: they race to plan a trip on the London Underground.

Answers
Take the yellow/Circle line or the green/District line to Victoria station. Change to the light blue/Victoria line and travel to Hyde Park Corner.

4 Read the timetable and answer in groups.
Students read a timetable and answer questions about it.

Answers
1. This timetable is for the Piccadilly line.
2. The color of this line on the map is dark blue.
3. No, this timetable is only valid from Mondays to Saturdays.
4. It leaves at 5:23 a.m. on a weekday.

Stop and Think! Critical Thinking
How can you be respectful to people on public transportation?
- Read the *Stop and Think!* box aloud and ask students to share their ideas.
- Students can talk to a partner about what they can do to be respectful of others while using public transportation.
- After a few minutes, bring the class together and discuss their ideas.

Wrap-up
Students practice writing directions.
- Have students race to give directions to Blackfriars Station from Paddington Station.
- Students write the directions on a piece of paper or in their notebooks. When students finish, have them raise their hands. The first student to finish and give correct directions wins.
- Check answers as a class.

➡ **(No homework today.)**

 **Project**

> **Objectives**
> Students will be able to use **transportation** vocabulary to write a proposal about eco-friendly means of transportation.

Lesson 9   Student's Book p. 36

Warm-up
Students discuss transportation in their community.
- Ask students to name the kinds of public transportation they have in their city or town. Elicit answers from students.
- Ask students if other forms of transportation are more popular, and why or why not.

1 Work in pairs. Complete the table about the means of transportation in your city.
Students work in pairs to describe the transportation in their city.
- Have students work in pairs.
- Ask students to complete the table to describe the transportation in their city.
- Direct students' attention to the **Glossary** box. Note that *eco-friendly* means it causes less harm to the environment than other means of transportation. *Fossil fuels* means fuels derived from coal or oil, like gasoline.
- Students give their opinions of each form of transportation in their town and describe the ecological (environmental) impact by circling the icon for uses *fossil fuel* or *eco-friendly*. Then students should fill in the number of stars for their rating. One star is not good, and five stars are very good.

Answers

In my town Answers will vary.
Ecological impact [top to bottom] fossil fuel, eco-friendly, fossil fuel, fossil fuel, fossil fuel, fossil fuel, fossil fuel, Answers will vary.

2 Work with a partner to answer the questions.
Students discuss the modes of transportation in their city in pairs.
- Ask students to discuss the questions and take notes.
- Explain that their answers will be part of their project.

Answers

Answers will vary.

3 Brainstorm a new, eco-friendly means of transportation.
Students complete a table with ideas for a new means of transportation that will be less harmful to the environment.

Wrap-up
Students review each other's ideas for a new form of transportation.
- Have pairs exchange their tables with each other and read each other's work.
- After a few minutes, have pairs ask and answer questions about their ideas.
- Encourage students to be respectful of each other's work and to offer each other constructive criticism.

Lesson 10   Student's Book pp. 36 and 37

Warm-up
Students discuss eco-friendly means of transportation.
- Write vocabulary for different means of transportation on the board.
- Ask students to vote on whether each form of transportation is eco-friendly or not. Students raise their hands to vote.
- Count the votes for each means of transportation and write the number on the board.

4 Create a poster to present your proposal.
Students create a poster to present their proposals for a new form of eco-friendly transportation from yesterday's lesson.
- Have students work in the same pairs as they did in the previous class.
- Ask students to review their notes on their ideas on a new eco-friendly means of transportation.
- Ask students to create a poster for their proposal. Students use the information in their notes and in the table on page 36. Invite students to be creative and use colorful pictures.
- Draw students' attention to the photo and poster on page 37. They can use this as a model for their own posters.

5 Present your proposal to your classmates.
Students present their proposals and posters to the class.
- Have each pair complete the sentences on page 37 with their own information.
- Draw students' attention to the *Tips* box on page 36. Read the information aloud and allow students to practice their presentations. Remind students that they should not read their presentations to the class.
- Ask each pair of students to present their posters to the class. Allow a few minutes at the end of each presentation for students to ask questions.

The Digital Touch
To incorporate digital media in the project, suggest one or more of the following:
- Students can create posters online at www.postermywall.com.
- Students can use software like Word or Google Docs to format and make the text for their posters.

Note that students should have the option to do a task on paper or digitally.

Wrap-up
Students vote on the most eco-friendly proposal.
- Ask students to do a secret vote to decide which proposal is the most eco-friendly. A secret vote will help students feel more confident about their own work.
- Have each student write the name of the proposal they choose on a small piece of paper. Students should fold their papers and hand them to you.
- Count the votes and announce the winner.

 **Workbook p. 132, Activities 1 and 2 (Review)**

Teaching Tip
Establishing a Respectful Atmosphere
Students may get nervous when they give presentations. It is important to make students feel safe in the classroom and to know that they will not be made fun of. Be aware of the atmosphere in the classroom—if students need extra support to calm their nerves, try to guide their presentation by asking questions.

Review

Objectives
Students will be able to use **places in the city** and **transportation** vocabulary as well as **imperatives** and **irregular comparatives and superlatives**.

Lesson 11   Student's Book pp. 38 and 39

✔ **Homework Check!**
Workbook p. 132, Activities 1 and 2 (Review)

Answers
1 Correct the sentences.
1. ~~bank~~ You can buy a soda at a <u>convenience store</u>.
2. ~~far~~ My school is <u>farther</u> than the mall.
3. ~~school~~ You can buy vegetables at a <u>supermarket</u>.
4. ~~cross~~ Walk straight and <u>turn</u> left at the hospital.

2 In your notebook, write your opinion.
Answers will vary.

Warm-up

Students review words for places in a city by unscrambling and correcting vocabulary items.

- Write the following on the board: 1. convenience market, 2. superstore, 3. drugshop, 4. coffee market.
- Have students race to correct the places in a city.

Answers
1. convenience store, 2. supermarket, 3. drugstore, 4. coffee shop

1 Number the pictures. What place does each picture suggest?
Students review words for places in a city by matching photos with the place each is associated with.

Answers
left to right, top to bottom 6, 5, 4, 7, 3, 2, 8, 1

2 Look and label.
Students review vocabulary for transportation by labeling photos of different means of transportation.

Answers
1. bus, 2. train, 3. motorcycle, 4. subway, 5. car, 6. plane, 7. bicycle, 8. taxi

3 Draw signs for the instructions.
Students draw signs to express the instructions.

Answers
1. [arrow pointing left], 2. [picture of person walking with diagonal line through it], 3. [stop sign], 4. [arrow pointing right with a diagonal line through it]

Wrap-up
Students race to review vocabulary for places in a city.
- Write the following questions on the board:
  » Where do you buy food? (Supermarket)
  » Where do you put money? (Bank)
  » Where do you sit on a bench? (Park)
  » Where can you buy clothes? (Mall)
- Elicit answers from students.

▶ **(No homework today.)**

Lesson 12   Student's Book p. 39

Warm-up

Students review irregular comparative forms.

- Write the following sentences on the board with gaps for students to fill:

  » *The subway is _____ than the bus.*

  » *Cars are ____ than buses.*

- Ask students to fill in the blanks with an irregular comparative form (*better, worse*). Call on volunteers to share their answers and to give reasons for them.
- Ask students if they agree or disagree.

4 Complete the chart.

Students complete the chart with irregular comparative and superlative forms.

Answers

good better, best; *bad* worse, worst, *far* farther, farthest

5 Write sentences using the comparative form.

Students practice using irregular comparative forms by writing sentences from cues.

Answers

1. Willow Park is farther from downtown than Green Park is.
2. CSB Drugstore is better than Willow Drugstore.
3. Planet Coffee Shop is worse than Awesome Coffee Shop.
4. Emma's middle school is farther from her house than her primary school is.

6 Write four sentences in your notebook using the superlative form. Use the information in the chart.

Students practice using irregular superlative forms by writing sentences based on the information in the chart.

- Note that one star is a negative review and five stars is a great review.

Answers

1. Roasted is the worst coffee shop.
2. Carla's Coffee is the best coffee shop.
3. T-Mart is the worst supermarket.
4. Food Boutique is the best supermarket.

? Big Question

Students are given the opportunity to revisit the Big Question and reflect on it.

- Tell students to turn to the unit opener on page 29.
- Split students into small groups.
- Ask students to discuss the Big Question: *How do you get around?* Remind students to think about the vocabulary (transportation and places in a city) and the theme of this unit (travel).
- After 5 minutes of discussion, bring the conversation back to the whole class. Ask groups to share their ideas. Do students agree or disagree?

★ Scorecard

Hand out (and/or project) a *Scorecard*. Have students fill in their *Scorecards* for this unit.

▸ **Study for the unit test.**

3 What makes a good friend?

Grammar	Vocabulary
Present simple: A good friend <u>helps</u> you. Good friends <u>don't argue</u> a lot. <u>Do</u> your friends <u>listen</u> to you? **Present continuous:** Ethan <u>is watching</u> a movie. We <u>are not playing</u> soccer. <u>Are</u> they <u>talking</u> about me?	**Physical Description:** blond, chubby, long, medium height, medium weight, short, thin **Personality:** funny, intelligent, kind, outgoing, rude, serious, shy

Listening	Writing
Identifying speaker's attitude	Completing a form

What makes a good friend?

In the first lesson, read the unit title aloud and have students look carefully at the unit cover. Encourage them to think about the message in the picture. At the end of the unit, students will discuss the big question: *What makes a good friend?*

 Teaching Tip

Activating Previous Knowledge
When you preview a unit, you can also have students look at the different pictures and headings in the unit. You can ask students what they already know and what they think they will learn. You can also ask what they would like to learn in this unit.

 **Vocabulary**

Objective
Students will be able to use **appearance** and **personality** vocabulary in descriptions.

Lesson 1 Student's Book p. 42

Warm-up
Students discuss what they think makes a good friend.
- Put students in small groups.
- Ask *What makes a good friend?*
- Have students brainstorm the qualities of a good friend. Students should make a list of the different qualities.
- After five minutes, come back together as a class and share answers.

1 Look at the picture and describe the girl.
Students practice appearance vocabulary by describing the girl in the picture.
- Draw students' attention to the **Guess What!** box. Read the information aloud and ask when they use avatars. (For example, in video games, on social networking sites, etc.)

2 🎧¹⁰ **Listen and mark (✓) the correct option.**
Students listen to the audio describing different people and choose which description matches the girl in the picture.

Answer

Description 2

Audio Script
1. My avatar is short and chubby. She has short blond hair and blue eyes. She wears braces.
2. My avatar is tall and thin. She has long brown hair and brown eyes.
3. My avatar is medium height and medium weight. She has short dark hair and dark eyes. She wears glasses.

Wrap-up
Students create avatars.
- Tell students to draw an avatar. Using appearance vocabulary from this lesson, students then write their descriptions in their notebooks.
- Have students form small groups.
- Students share their descriptions, making corrections if necessary.

 **Workbook p. 134, Activities 1–3**

💭 **Teaching Tip**
Avoiding Awkwardness
In some cases, you may want to avoid having students describe each other. Get an idea of the way students interact with each other. If they are generally friendly with each other, then they may be able to describe each other. But if they show any signs of bullying, or if they are not as friendly towards each other, avoid asking them to describe each other.

Lesson 2 — Student's Book p. 43

✔ **Homework Check!**

Workbook p. 134, Activities 1–3

Answers

1 Use the words from the box to complete the mind maps.
Eye color blue, brown, dark, green
Other braces, glasses
Body medium height, medium weight, short, tall, thin

2 Circle the correct option. Then write the name of the movie.
0. ... has, have, 1. am, have, wear, has, is, has, *Despicable Me*, 2. am, have, is, has, *How to Train Your Dragon*, 3. am, have, have, wears, has, *Inside Out*

3 Complete the description.
She is tall and chubby. She has blond hair and green eyes.

Warm-up
Students review vocabulary for describing appearance.
- Students form pairs.
- Student A describes a friend. Student B draws the friend based on the description. Student A says if the drawing matches the description or not.
- Students switch roles. Now Student B describes a friend and Student A draws.

3 Complete the descriptions of the avatars.
Students complete the sentences using appearance vocabulary.

Answers
1. short, short, 2. thin, blond, eyes

4 Think Fast! Describe the other two avatars.
Students do a two-minute timed challenge: they describe pictures 3 and 4 of SoccerJim and MrTie.

Answers
Answers will vary.

5 Complete the descriptions using the avatar names.
Students are exposed to words for describing personalities as they identify which avatar goes with each person.

Answers
1. MsSunshine, 2. MrTie, 3. K-Man, 4. SoccerJim

6 🎧 Listen and number.
Students match personality traits to people based on an audio.

Answers
from top to bottom 3 *rude*, 1 *shy*, 4 *intelligent*, 2 *funny*

Audio Script
1. Jesse
GIRL: So, you're Jesse, right?
BOY: Uh… yes, I am.
GIRL: And you're a new student here, I guess.
BOY: Uh… yes.
GIRL: And are you enjoying the school?
BOY: Uh-huh.
GIRL: I see. Listen, we can play video games together some day.
BOY: Nice…

2. Will
BOY 1: Hey guys, listen to another one. What is the monster's favorite cheese?
BOY 2: Hmm… I don't know…
GIRL: I have no idea.
BOY 3: Me neither!
BOY 1: It's "monsterella!"

3. Olivia
GIRL 1: Come on, Anna! Hurry up! I don't have all day!
GIRL 2: Hey, Olivia, take it easy…
GIRL 1: Why should I take it easy? You're so slow!
GIRL 2: Oh, Olivia…

4. Luke
BOY 1: Wow, Luke! You got an A in all subjects!
BOY 2: Yep.
BOY 1: Congrats! That's amazing! The history test was so difficult!
BOY 2: Nah… it was OK… I can help you study if you like.

Stop and Think! Critical Thinking
Describe a friend.
- Students can now add to their descriptions of their friends from the warm-up activity in this lesson. Tell students to work in the same pairs and take turns describing their friends' personalities.

Wrap-up
Students expand on personality vocabulary.
- Draw students' attention to the **Guess What!** box. Read the information aloud and ask students to replace the adjectives in Activity 5 with opposite words, if possible.
- Ask what kinds of avatars these people would have now that they have opposite personalities.

➡ **Workbook p. 135, Activities 4–6**

 Grammar

Objective
Students will be able to use **present simple** and **present continuous** to talk about friendship.

Lesson 3   Student's Book p. 44

✔ **Homework Check!**
Workbook p. 135, Activities 4–6

Answers
4 Complete the words using *a, e, i, o, u* and *y*.
1. kind, 2. funny, 3. rude, 4. serious, 5. intelligent, 6. shy
5 Read the review and complete the sentences.
1. funny, 2. popular, 3. shy, 4. intelligent
6 Write your opinions.
Answers will vary.

 46 **Warm-up**

Students review the present simple form while completing sentences so they are true for them.
- Write the following statements on the board:
  I _____ (play, +/–) video games.
  My friends _____ (play, +/–) soccer.
  Have students write the sentences in their notebooks so that they are true for them (filling in the gap with *play* or *don't play*).
- As a class, compare answers. Have students who play video games stand in one part of the room, and those who do not play video games stand in another part of the room. Then do the same for the second sentence.

1 Read and circle the correct option.
Students practice the affirmative and negative present simple as they choose the options that best complete the sentences about friends.

Answers
1. helps, 2. don't argue, 3. doesn't tell, 4. feels, 5. respects, 6. don't get

2 Write sentences in affirmative (✓) or negative (✗).
Students write sentences in the affirmative or negative present simple using cues.

Answers
1. Jack and Connor don't have any secrets.
2. Emily agrees with Mia. 3. Carlos doesn't like Saul's friends. 4. Mason and Sue help each other solve problems.

Wrap-up
Students write a group story about friendship.
- Write the words *argue, get jealous, play, help, tell, feel* and *respect* on the board.
- Separate students into small groups.
- Tell each group to create a story about friendship using a sentence for each word on the board.
- Each student writes one sentence using one of the verbs. Then the next student writes the next sentence using another verb. Students continue until they have a short story using each verb in a sentence. Encourage students to use affirmative and negative forms.
- Bring the class back together and have each group share their stories.

➡ **Workbook p. 136, Activity 1**

Teaching Tip
Creating Meaningful Practice
When practicing verb forms, encourage students to use the verb forms in conversation (for example, in group discussions or in pair work). Using the grammar in spoken conversation can help students be more spontaneous with the language they use, making their use of the language more meaningful and memorable.

Lesson 4 — Student's Book p. 45

✔ **Homework Check!**
Workbook p. 136, Activity 1

Answers
1 Circle the correct words.
MR. DALE: Marianne, <u>do</u> you <u>have</u> a best friend?
MARIANNE: Yes, I <u>do</u>. Riley is my best friend.
MR. DALE: I see. And what <u>do</u> you <u>do</u> together?
MARIANNE: Well…we <u>listen</u> to music and <u>study</u> French.
MR. DALE: Nice…now, about the summer program. Why <u>do</u> you <u>want</u> to participate?
MARIANNE: I <u>want</u> to spend a month in Quebec because I <u>love</u> the language.
MR. DALE: And <u>do</u> your parents <u>oppose</u> the idea?
MARIANNE: Oh, no, they <u>don't</u>. Actually, they are very enthusiastic about it.
MR. DALE: That's great! Thanks, Marianne.

Warm-up
Students correct affirmative and negative present simple sentences.
- Write the following sentences on the board:
  I doesn't play video games.
  Tom and Lisa helps each other.
  We don't runs often.
  Do you plays soccer?
- Have students work in groups to correct the sentences. The first group to correct all of the sentences wins. (Answers: I <u>don't</u> play video games. Tom and Lisa <u>help</u> each other. We don't <u>run</u> often. Do you <u>play</u> soccer?)

3 Look and circle the correct options.
Students complete present continuous sentences with the correct form of the verb *be*.
- Draw students' attention to the **Simple vs. Continuous** box at the bottom of the page and read the information aloud. Note that in the previous lesson, we used the present simple (*I <u>play</u> video games*). Here, we will use the present continuous (*I <u>am playing</u> video games*).

Answers
1. are, 2. I'm, 3. is, are, 4. are

4 Read and number.
Students are exposed to questions in present continuous as they match each question to the correct response.

Answers
top to bottom 4, 3, 1, 2

5 Think Fast! Mime activities for classmates to guess.
Students do a one-minute timed challenge: they review verbs for activities by acting out the activities while classmates guess each activity.

Extension
Students work in pairs to describe photo 1, 3 or 4 on page 45. Tell students to write a sentence for each action they see, this time using the present simple. Students should also describe each person in the photo, using vocabulary from this unit for appearance and personality.

Wrap-up
Students look at the illustrations on page 44 and describe each scene using the present continuous.
- Have students work in small groups.
- Have groups race to write a description of each picture. Each picture gets a separate round.
- When a group finishes their description, students should raise their hands.
- The first group to complete each picture description correctly with the present continuous gets a point. The group with the most points at the end wins.

➡ **Workbook p. 136, Activity 2**

Listening & Writing

Objectives
Students will be able to identify reasons a speaker gives. Students will also be able to complete a form.

Lesson 5   Student's Book pp. 46 and 47

✔ **Homework Check!**
Workbook p. 136, Activity 2

Answers
2 Write questions and answers using present continuous.
1. Is Chloe studying French too? No, she isn't studying French.
2. Are you wearing a uniform? Yes, I'm wearing a uniform.
3. Where are you walking? I'm walking to school.
4. Is Bob playing video games? No, he's watching TV.

Warm-up
Students review the present continuous and the present simple.
- Write the following sentences with blank spaces on the board: *Kim and Sarah _____ video games often. / Kim and Sarah _____ video games right now.*
- Have students complete the sentences in their notebooks individually, using the verb *play* in the present simple or present continuous. Be sure to ask why students chose their answers.

Answers
play, are playing

1 ¹² **Listen and identify the poster.**
Students listen to the audio and identify which poster it goes with.

Answer
Canada Summer Program

Audio Script
Attention please, for a special announcement. Do you like to travel? Do you like to study French? We are organizing a one-month summer school program in Quebec, Canada. You'll study French and live with a Canadian family. Our school is offering two free trips. You can get one of them! Apply before March 23. Please look for me for more information. I am Mr. Dale, the school counselor.

2 Complete the information on the poster.
Students complete the poster with information from the audio.

Answers
French, Canadian, 23

Extension
- Ask students the names of cities they would like to visit and write them on the board.
- Separate students into groups based on where they would like to go. Tell students to come up with five activities they would like to do in that city.
- Have students write complete sentences using the present simple to describe the activities. Then have students share their sentences with the class.

Wrap-up
Students listen to the audio again and identify examples of the present continuous.
- Play the audio from Activity 1 again.
- Tell students to raise their hands when they hear the present continuous.
- Have students identify the present continuous verbs they hear and use them in a sentence.

Answers
are organizing, is offering

▶ **Workbook p. 137, Activity 1**

🐝 **Teaching Tip**
Managing Fast Finishers
Some students complete activities more quickly than others, so it's a good idea to have a few extra activities on hand, otherwise these students may become bored and disruptive. One set of activities designed for fast finishers are the *Just for Fun* pages. Students can work on these individually and then check their answers in the back of the Student's Book. The *Just for Fun* activities for this unit are on page 54.

Lesson 6
Student's Book pp. 46 and 47

> ✔ **Homework Check!**
> Workbook p. 137, Activity 1
>
> **Answers**
> **1 Read the text. Then mark (✓) *Manga* and/or *Anime*.**
> 1. Anime, 2. Manga, 3. Anime, 4. Manga, 5. Manga and Anime

Warm-up
Draw students' attention to the **Guess What!** box. Read the information aloud and ask students to answer the question *Why do you like English?* for themselves. Elicit answers from students using *because*.

3 🎧¹³ **Listen and mark (✓) the correct answers.**
Students listen to the audio and identify the reasons the speakers give.

Answers

1. Because she likes to study French and she wants to learn about Canadian culture. 2. Because she wants to have fun in Montreal and she thinks Canada is a cool country.

Audio Script
Riley
Mr. Dale: So Riley, your grades in French are excellent! Do you like studying French?
Riley: Yes, I do, Mr. Dale. It's my favorite subject.
Mr. Dale: Right. Good grades are important for this summer program. Why do you like French?
Riley: Because my grandfather is from France, and he speaks French. Also because learning a foreign language is very important for my future.
Mr. Dale: I see. And why do you want to participate in the summer program?
Riley: Uh… Because I really want to improve my speaking skills and learn about Canadian culture.
Mr. Dale: Nice.
Chloe
Mr. Dale: So Chloe… Your grades in French are not very good… Do you like studying French?
Chloe: Yes, I do, Mr. Dale, but it's not my favorite subject. I prefer history.
Mr. Dale: OK... And tell me, Chloe, why do you want to participate in the summer program?
Chloe: Because I think Canada is a cool country! And because I want to have fun in Montreal.
Mr. Dale: I see.

4 Fill out the form.
In a personalization activity, students complete the form with information that is true for them.

Answers
Answers will vary.

Stop and Think! Critical Thinking
What can you learn by studying in another country?
- Tell students to share their answers to Activity 4 with a partner.
- Draw students' attention to the **Stop and Think!** box and read the text aloud. Ask students what they could learn by studying in Canada, for example.
- Have students discuss their answers in pairs, using their answers to Activity 4 to help them.

Wrap-up
Students interview each other for a study abroad program.
- Invite students to imagine they have applied to a program to study in the United States.
- Tell students to work in pairs to interview each other for the program.
- Students should use the audio in Activity 4 as a model.
- Have students take turns interviewing each other and taking notes on each other's answers.

➡ **Workbook p. 137, Activity 2**

Preparing for the Next Lesson
Ask students to watch an introduction to cosplay: goo.gl/dgxEkq.

 Culture

Objectives
Students will be able to explore cosplay and talk about reasons people enjoy hobbies.

Lesson 7   Student's Book pp. 48 and 49

> ✔ **Homework Check!**
> Workbook p. 137, Activity 2
>
> **Answers**
> **2 Create your own character. Copy the table in your notebook.**
> Answers will vary.

Warm-up
Tell students to look at the pictures on pages 48 and 49. Have them form pairs and discuss with their partner.
- Ask student pairs *What do you see in the pictures? What culture(s) do the pictures show? What can you learn about that culture from these pictures?*

1 **Read the encyclopedia entry. Then circle T (True) or F (False).**
Students read the text and determine whether statements about the topic are true or false based on the encyclopedia entry.

Answers
1. F, *Cosplay* is the combination of two other words.
2. T, 3. F, Cosplayers exchange cards at meetings and events. 4. T

2 **Think Fast! Look and identify: an anime illustration, a *meishi* card and a picture of cosplay from fantasy, history and video games.**
Students do a one-minute timed challenge: they identify the items listed on pages 48 and 49.

> ### Extension
> Students personalize the discussion of cosplay.
> - Encourage students to think about their favorite characters from video games, history and fantasy. Which ones would they choose to cosplay?
> - Have students discuss in pairs. Tell students to describe the character's physical traits and personality using vocabulary from this unit.

Wrap-up
Students create a *meishi* (business card) for a cosplay character.
- Ask students to think about a character they would use for cosplay. Have them think about how they would describe their characters to another person. (If the class did the Extension activity, they can use the same characters.)
- Students draw their character on a piece of paper or on an index card.
- Have students write important characteristics or traits for the character on the card. For example, *bald, warrior, strong,* etc.
- Have students exchange their meishi cards with their classmates.

➡ **(No homework today.)**

 50

Lesson 8   Student's Book pp. 48 and 49

Warm-up
Students practice appearance and personality vocabulary while reviewing the topic.
- Students form small groups.
- Tell students to think of three adjectives for appearance or personality to describe each person in the pictures on pages 48 and 49.
- After five minutes, student groups share their answers with the class. Ask students if they agree on their answers.

3 🎧¹⁴ **Listen and answer. Why does Midori like cosplay?**
Students listen to the audio and answer the questions.
- Draw students' attention to the **Guess What!** box. Read the information aloud and ask *Would you buy or make your cosplay costume? Why?*

Answers

1. manga, 2. another person, 3. new friends

Audio Script
Hi! My name's Midori and I'm from Nagoya, Japan. I like cosplay for three reasons.
First, because I love manga—I always attend cosplay meetings and conventions here in Japan. I dress up as different characters.
Secondly, because I love to dress up and become another person: the costume, the wig, the shoes, the makeup… I spend hours getting ready, and it's a lot of fun. I am a very shy person, but I become more outgoing and friendly when I'm wearing my outfit. And thirdly, because I have fantastic friends in the cosplay community. We like the same things and have a lot of fun together. Cosplay makes me feel good, and I am more sociable. It's easy to make new friends when you are a cosplay character. Cosplay is great!

4 Answer *Yes, she does* or *No, she doesn't.*
Students give short answers to questions about the audio.

Answers

1. No, she doesn't. 2. No, she doesn't. 3. No, she doesn't. 4. No, she doesn't.

Stop and Think! Critical Thinking
Do you need to be really good at a hobby to enjoy it?
- Ask students *What are some hobbies you can think of?* Elicit answers from the class and note ideas on the board.
- Then ask *Why do people enjoy these hobbies?* Encourage students to give reasons using *Because they…*
- Ask *Can people enjoy their hobbies for these reasons even if they aren't really good at them?* To promote discussion, divide the class into two groups, one who will argue *Yes, they can* and the other, who will be assigned to argue *No, they can't*.

Wrap-up
Students compare hobbies and ask and answer questions.
- Students work in new pairs. Ask *What is your hobby?*
- Have students ask and answer questions about each other's hobbies.
- Write the following questions on the board: *Why do you like your hobby? Are you really good at it? What do you like most about your hobby?*
- Have students take turns asking and answering the questions. If there is time, students can present their partner's hobbies to the class.

 **(No homework today.)**

🐝 Teaching Tip
Encouraging Longer Answers
Challenge students to expand on their answers. For example, in Activity 4, ask students to give more information about why Midori does or does not do something.

Project

Objective
Students will be able to make a self-esteem kit.

Lesson 9 Student's Book p. 50

Warm-up
Students review personality vocabulary.
- Tell students to look at the words in the cloud in Activity 1. In small groups, have them use each word to describe someone or something in a sentence.
- The first group to finish using the correct meanings wins.

1 Organize the words from the cloud in the chart.

Students categorize personality vocabulary as *Positive*, *Neutral* or *Negative*.

Answers
Positive funny, intelligent, kind, outgoing
Neutral serious, shy
Negative rude

Stop and Think! Critical Thinking
How do people feel when you use negative words to describe them?
- Draw students' attention to the **Stop and Think!** box and read the question aloud.
- Have students discuss their opinions in small groups.
- Note that sometimes hearing negative words can hurt people's feelings, so we need to be careful with the words we use to describe people.

2 Look and number the thought bubbles.

Students read the thought bubbles and number them to match them to the picture that illustrates each thought.

Answers
from top to bottom 4, 3, 2, 1

Wrap-up
Students expand on how descriptions can make people feel.
- Students work in pairs.
- Tell students to imagine they are acting the part of a cosplay character with two or more of the personality traits listed on page 50.
- Tell pairs to make sure each student chooses different personality traits.
- Student A describes his or her character (briefly).
- Student B disagrees with Student A (while both remain in character): *No, you're not kind. You're rude.*
- Students switch roles and repeat.

➡ **(No homework today.)**

Lesson 10 Student's Book p. 51

Warm-up

Students review positive, negative and neutral words for describing people.
- Have students close their books.
- Write the words from the box on page 50 on the board.
- Tell students to identify the negative words. Have a volunteer cross them out.
- Invite another volunteer to circle the positive words.

3 Make a self-care kit.

Students create a self-esteem kit that will make them feel better when they are sad.
- Draw students' attention to the **Tips!** box at the bottom of the page. Ask a volunteer to read the text aloud.
- Tell students follow Step 2 to write their lists.
- Have students compare their lists with a partner. Ask *Are your lists similar or different? How?*
- Put students in small groups. Ask *How will the items on your lists make you feel better?* Have students take turns identifying the reasons for items on their lists to their groups.
- Tell students to assemble their self-care kits at home and bring them to class the next day.

The Digital Touch

To incorporate digital media in the project, suggest one or more of the following:
- Students can select items for their kit on the Internet and group them on a site like Pinterest or Tumblr.
- Students can find photos of items for their kits online and make a collage on a website like fotor.com or photocollage.net.

Note that students should have the option to do a task on paper or digitally.

Wrap-up

Students review appearance vocabulary words by describing the items in the pictures on page 51.
- Point at the pictures and ask *What do you see?* Elicit responses from students. Tell students to describe the physical appearance of the items in Step 3: *a thin brown bear*. Also, *someone's grandparents. They have gray hair. They are happy*.
- Tell students to describe what some of the items they will place in their self-care kits will look like, for example, photos, toys, food, etc.

➥ **Workbook p. 136, Activity 1 (Review)**

Review

Objective
Students will be able to consolidate their understanding of the vocabulary and grammar learned in the unit.

Lesson 11 — Student's Book p. 52

> ✔ **Homework Check!**
> Workbook p. 136, Activity 1 (Review)
> **Answers**
> 1 Answer about you and a friend in your notebook.
> Answers will vary.

Warm-up

Students review words for describing personality traits and physical traits.
- Write the words *shy, outgoing, tall* and *short* on the board.
- Ask for volunteers to draw or act out the word in front of the class and have the class guess each word.

1 Classify the words.
Students put the words into categories: *Hair, Body* and *Personality Traits*.

Answers
Hair black, blond, brown, long, short
Body chubby, short, tall, thin
Personality Traits intelligent, outgoing, rude, shy

2 Look and complete the descriptions.
Students look at the pictures and complete the descriptions of the people using the words from this unit.

Answers
1. tall, black, 2. weight, short, 3. medium, short, 4. blond, short, 5. thin, long

> **Extension**
> Students develop longer descriptions.
> - Students form pairs.
> - Tell students to work individually at first to think of at least one more appearance word to describe each of the friends in Activity 2.
> - Have students use each word in a sentence for each friend.
> - Working with their partners, students read each other their sentences and guess which friend each of their partner's sentences is describing.

Wrap-up

Students review words for personality traits.
- Students form small groups.
- Tell groups to look at the picture of the friends on page 52 and choose a personality trait to describe each person. Have students write their choices in their notebooks.
- Have each student tell their group which personality word they would use to describe each friend and give a reason for their choice: *Alan is serious because he is the only one who isn't smiling in the photo.*
- When groups finish, discuss the activity as a class. Did group members agree or disagree?

⏵ **(No homework today.)**

Lesson 12 Student's Book p. 53

Warm-up

Students review affirmative and negative verb forms in present simple and present continuous.
Write the following sentences on the board:
Karin plays soccer after school.
Roberto does not play video games.
Daniel and Thomas are walking home from school.
Stephen is not studying for his test.

- Have students label each sentence as affirmative or negative.
- Then ask students if the sentences use the present simple (routines, habits), or the present continuous (things happening now).
- Finally, have students rewrite the affirmative sentences as negative and vice versa in their notebooks.

3 Complete the sentences using the verb in the affirmative or negative form.

Students complete the sentences in present simple using the verb in parentheses in the affirmative or negative form.

Answers
1. respects, 2. don't criticize, 3. don't tell, 4. listens

4 Look at the pictures and write sentences.

Students use the present continuous to describe the pictures.

Answers
1. playing soccer. 2. is running. 3. He is reading a book. 4. They are having a picnic.

5 Write the complete questions.

Students write questions in present continuous using cues.

Answers
1. Are you playing video games? 2. Is Josh walking to school? 3. Is Ella playing soccer? 4. Are Tyler and Noah skateboarding?

 Big Question

Students are given the opportunity to revisit the Big Question and reflect on it.

- Tell students to turn to the unit opener on page 41 and read the Big Question, "What makes a good friend?"
- Students form small groups.
- Tell students to list the verbs in Activity 3 in their notebooks: *respect, criticize, tell (secrets), listen*. Then have them turn to page 44 and add the verbs they find there: *help, argue, feel (happy for you), get (jealous), have (secrets), agree, like*.
- Using their verb lists (with their books closed), have groups write sentences describing the qualities of a good friend.
- When groups finish, bring the conversation back to the whole class. Ask groups to share their sentences. Do students agree or disagree?

 Scorecard

Hand out (and/or project) a *Scorecard*. Have students fill in their *Scorecards* for this unit.

➡ **Study for the unit test.**

> ### Teaching Tip
> **Moving to Full-Class Discussion**
> Bringing a small group discussion back to a full-class discussion can open up the conversation to new ideas. Invite each group to share their ideas. Then ask each group if they agree or disagree with their classmates and why.

4 What do we eat?

Grammar	Vocabulary
Countable and uncountable nouns: We have two <u>carrots</u> and some <u>broccoli</u>. **Quantifiers:** *some, any*: There is <u>some</u> rice, but there aren't <u>any</u> onions. Is there <u>any</u> juice?	**Food and Drinks:** apple, banana, beans, beef, bread, broccoli, butter, carrot, cheese, chicken, egg, fish, juice, milk, onions, oranges, pasta, rice, soda, water

Reading	Speaking
Identifying main ideas	Recommending a restaurant

What do we eat?

In the first lesson, read the unit title aloud and have students look carefully at the unit cover. Encourage them to think about the message in the picture. At the end of the unit, students will discuss the big question: *What do we eat?*

 Teaching Tip

Guiding Pair and Group Discussions

Small group and pair discussions give students more opportunities to speak English in the classroom. Try to give students some time to speak to each other each class. You can check their work by walking around the room and listening in. You can also join the conversations.

 Vocabulary

Objective
Students will be able to use **food and drinks** vocabulary to talk about their preferences.

Lesson 1   Student's Book pp. 56 and 57

Warm-up

Students preview the unit and the Big Question.
- Have students work in small groups.
- Tell students to look through the pages in the unit.
- Ask *What foods do you eat?*
- Have students circle the pictures of food that they eat in the unit.

1 Write the food items in the correct category.
Students are introduced to food and drinks vocabulary and categories.
- Draw students' attention to the food chart.
- Tell them to write the food items in the correct categories.
- Draw students' attention to the **Guess What!** box. Read the information aloud and ask students what foods they have for breakfast, lunch and dinner. Ask *Do you have dessert?*

Answers
Fruit oranges, *Grains* rice, *Protein* beans, *Vegetables* onions, *Dairy* milk, *Drinks* water

2 ¹⁵ Listen and check.
Students listen to the audio and check their answers to Activity 1.

Audio Script
Hi! My name is Isabella. Food items can be divided into five groups: fruits, vegetables, grains, protein and dairy. Including items from these groups in your diet is good for you! Let's see the items in each group.
Fruit… There are apples, bananas and oranges. I like oranges a lot!
Vegetables… There's broccoli, there are carrots and there are onions. Carrots are delicious!
Protein… Beef, chicken, eggs, fish and beans. I don't really like fish.
Grains… examples are bread, pasta and rice. Pasta is delicious, but I don't like rice very much.
Dairy… butter, cheese and milk. I don't like butter at all! Yuck!
Drinks… Most people like to have a drink with their meals. Some options are juice and water.

3 Listen again and complete the sentences.
Students listen to the audio and complete the sentences with the food and drinks vocabulary they hear.

Answers
1. oranges, carrots, pasta, 2. fish, rice, butter

Wrap-up
Students review food and drink vocabulary while discussing which foods are eaten at which meals.
- Draw a table with three columns on the board: *Breakfast*, *Lunch*, *Dinner*.
- Tell students to choose a meal for each food and drink item on pages 56 and 57.
- If students disagree which meal an item goes with, ask their reasons for choosing a particular meal.

➡ **Workbook p. 138, Activity 1**

Lesson 2 — Student's Book p. 57

> ✔ **Homework Check!**
> Workbook p. 138, Activity 1
>
> **Answers**
> **1 Look at the pictures and solve the puzzle. What is the mystery food?**
> 1. cheese, 2. fish, 3. juice, 4. milk, 5. egg, 6. beans, *vertical* chicken

Warm-up
Students review food and drinks vocabulary from the previous lesson.
- Write the names of different foods and drinks students learned in Lesson 1 on the board.
- Have students close their books.
- Ask students to match the words to the correct category: *fruit, vegetables, grains, drinks, protein* or *dairy*.

4 🎧¹⁶ **Listen and mark (✓) what they eat and drink.**
Students listen to the audio and mark what the speakers eat and drink.

Answers

Lucas beans, chicken, rice, tomatoes, water
Abby apple, fish, carrots, rice, orange juice

Audio Script
1. Lucas
Lunch is my favorite meal. I usually eat at home: we often have chicken and rice, and we have beans. We normally eat a salad with lots of tomatoes; I love tomatoes. And I always have a glass of water.
2. Abby
I have dinner at my grandma's house, and she's a great cook! We usually have rice and we eat fish. We also eat boiled vegetables, especially carrots, because I like them a lot. I have fresh, homemade orange juice and I eat an apple for dessert.

5 Think Fast! Say three food items you like and two you don't like.
Students do a one-minute timed challenge: they tell their partners three foods they like and two foods they don't like.

6 Complete the table with your ideas.
Students categorize food and drink vocabulary words in the table to describe their likes and habits.

Stop and Think! Critical Thinking
Why do we eat and drink things we don't like?
- Draw students' attention to the **Stop and Think!** box and read the information aloud.
- Invite students to share the food items in the second column of the table they completed in Activity 6.
- Write students' answers on the board.
- Ask *Why do you eat these foods or drink these drinks even though you don't like them?* Elicit answers.
- Then ask *Do these foods and drinks have anything in common?* Students should come to understand that sometimes we have to eat foods we don't like because they are healthy for us. They help us grow and stay strong.

> **Extension**
> Tell students to find someone who has similar likes and habits. Have students go around the room and find students who have the same answers or similar answers.

Wrap-up
Write the names of different foods and drinks on the board, one by one. Survey students for their opinions, likes and dislikes about each food or drink.
- For example, write the word *broccoli* on the board. Ask *Do you like and eat broccoli?*
- Tell students to stand on the left side of the room if they like and eat broccoli. Ask students to stand on the right side of the room if they don't like and eat broccoli. Ask students to stand at the back of the room if they don't like and don't eat broccoli.
- Ask each group to discuss their answers together. After two minutes, elicit answers from a representative of each group.

➡ **Workbook p. 138, Activities 2 and 3**

> 🐝 **Teaching Tip**
> **Modeling Activities**
> Remember to model activities for students before they begin. This helps to clarify expectations so they know exactly what they should do.

Grammar

Objectives
Students will be able to distinguish between **countable and uncountable nouns** and use **quantifiers** to talk about amounts of food and drink.

Lesson 3 Student's Book p. 58

✔ **Homework Check!**
Workbook p. 138, Activities 2 and 3

Answers
2 Circle the word that does not belong.
1. fish, Fish isn't a vegetable. 2. pasta, Pasta isn't a dairy product. 3. rice, Rice doesn't have protein. 4. bread, Bread isn't a drink. 5. onion, Onion isn't a fruit.
3 Write the words in the chart.
Plant products broccoli, *Drinks and Plant products* orange juice, *Drinks* water, *Animal products* beef

▶ 60 Warm-up
Students preview the grammar while reviewing food and drinks vocabulary.
- Write the following sentences on the board: *I have an apple. I have some milk. Alex has an apple. Alex has a cup of milk.*
- Read the sentences aloud to the class. Ask students to replace *apple/apples* with another food word, and *milk* with another drink word.

1 Read the recipe and classify the ingredients in your notebook.
Students practice identifying countable and uncountable nouns.
- Draw students' attention to the **Countable vs. Uncountable** box and read the sentences.
- Ask *Can you count bananas? Can you count sugar?* Elicit answers from the class.
- Tell students to create a two-column chart in their notebooks. One heading should read *Countable* and the other *Uncountable*.
- Have students read the recipe and classify the ingredients.

Answers
Countable nouns egg, banana
Uncountable nouns butter, milk, brown sugar, flour, baking powder

2 Look again at Activity 1, page 56. Add four items to the table in your notebook.
Students categorize the food and drink vocabulary as countable or uncountable nouns.

Answers
Countable nouns oranges, onions, apples, carrots, eggs
Uncountable nouns milk, beans, rice, water, broccoli, pasta, bread, beef, fish, chicken, cheese, juice

3 Mark the sentence + (affirmative), – (negative) or ? (a question).
Students are exposed to quantifiers while they determine whether sentences are affirmative, negative or questions.

Answers
1. – , 2. ? , 3. + , 4. ? , 5. + , 6. –

Wrap-up
Students review the use of *a/an*, *some* and *any* with countable and uncountable nouns.
- Write the following sentences on the board with blank spaces for the answers.
  Do you have _____ tomatoes?
  There is _____ tomato and _____ apple on the table.
  We need _____ milk for our cereal.
  There aren't _____ oranges left.
- Ask students to complete the sentences with *a/an*, *some* or *any* in their notebooks. The first student to answer correctly wins.

Answers
any, a, an, some, any

➡ **Workbook p. 139, Activities 1 and 2**

Lesson 4   Student's Book p. 59

✔ **Homework Check!**
Workbook p. 139, Activities 1 and 2
Answers
1 Classify the food in the table.
Countable nouns carrot, banana
Uncountable nouns pasta, broccoli, beef, juice
2 Mark the underlined words *C* (countable) or *U* (uncountable).
1. C, 2. C, 3. U, 4. U, 5. C, 6. C

Warm-up
Students review countable and uncountable nouns and *a/an*, *some* and *any*.
- Split students into small teams.
- Write the singular form of countable nouns and some uncountable nouns from this unit on the board, one at a time. For example, *apple, orange, milk, rice,* etc.
- As you write each word on the board, have student teams race to tell if the word is countable or uncountable. In order to get a point, students have to tell whether the word is countable or uncountable, then use it in a sentence correctly with *a/an*, *some* or *any*.

4 Complete the information.
Students practice using *a/an*, *any* and *some* with countable and uncountable nouns.
Answers
1. some, 2. any, 3. any, 4. a, 5. any, 6. some, 7. an

5 Complete the notes.
Students practice using countable and uncountable nouns while they complete the sentences.
- Draw students' attention to the **Guess What!** box. Read the information aloud and ask *Do you know of any other special food days?* Elicit answers from the class.
Answers
1. bananas, apple, orange, yogurt, 2. onion, tomatoes, beef, water, 3. apples, orange, egg, baking soda

6 🎧¹⁷ **Listen and mark ✓ (*There is/are some*) or ✗ (*There isn't/aren't any*).**
Students listen to the audio and mark whether the speakers have the ingredients listed.
Answers
eggs ✓ , *orange juice* ✓ , *flour* ✗, *apples* ✓, *baking soda* ✗

Audio Script
BOY: Let's make this Special Apple Pie!
GIRL: Good idea! Let's check if we have all the ingredients.
GIRL: Hmm… look! There are some eggs!
BOY: We need only one.
GIRL: Is there any orange juice?
BOY: Let me see… yes, there is some orange juice.
GIRL: Uh-oh… there isn't any flour!
BOY: No flour? And can you see any apples?
GIRL: Yes, there are some apples here.
BOY: OK. What about the baking soda?
GIRL: Baking soda? Hmm… there isn't any baking soda.
BOY: No flour, no baking soda… I can't make the apple pie today.
GIRL: That's too bad!

Wrap-up
Students review the use of *there is/are* and *there isn't any / aren't any* with countable and uncountable nouns.
- Group students into small teams.
- Write the following sentences on the board, one at a time, for students to correct.
  1. There is two apples on the table.
  2. There aren't any milk in the fridge.
  3. There isn't any oranges left.
  4. There are rice in the bowl.
- Students race to correct each sentence in a notebook for one point each. The team with the most points wins.
Answers
1. ~~is~~ are, 2. ~~aren't~~ isn't, 3. ~~isn't~~ aren't, 4. ~~are~~ is

 **Workbook pp. 139 and 140, Activities 3–5**

💭 Teaching Tip
Checking Each Other's Answers
A good way to help students take ownership of their learning is to have them check each other's answers. This will help them to internalize new grammar and vocabulary as they check their peers' work.

Reading & Speaking

Objectives
Students will be able to identify opinions. They will also be able to recommend a restaurant.

Lesson 5 Student's Book pp. 60 and 61

✔ **Homework Check!**
Workbook pp. 139 and 140, Activities 3–5

Answers
3 Read and draw.
Answers will vary.
4 Look. Then write sentences with *some* or *any*.
1. There are some eggs. 2. There is some milk. 3. There are some tomatoes. 4. There isn't any juice. 5. There are some carrots. 6. There isn't any soda.
5 Complete the conversations with *some*, *any*, *a* or *an*.
1. an, some, 2. some, some, some, any, 3. a, some, some, any, any

 62

Warm-up
Students preview the reading and theme for the lesson.
- Ask students to briefly glance at the text on the phone screens on page 60. Students should not read the text yet.
- Ask students what they think the text will be about.
- Ask students *Have you seen a text like this before? Where? What is its purpose?*

1 Look at the phone screens and circle T (True) or F (False).
Students read the text and determine whether the statements are true or false.
- Draw students' attention to the **Be Strategic!** box. Read the information aloud and ask students to read the text on the phone screens quickly to themselves.

Answers
1. T, 2. F (The restaurants are all different.), 3. T

2 Read the texts more carefully. Mark (✓) all the correct options.
Students read the texts more carefully for details and mark the restaurant(s) each statement is true for.

Answers
1. The Veggie Place, 2. Pampered Pizza, 3. Antonella's, Pampered Pizza, 4. Antonella's, 5. Sam's Diner

Wrap-up
Students talk about their preferences in restaurants.
- Write the names of each restaurant from the phone screens on the board.
- Take a class survey. Ask students to vote on the restaurants they would want to go to the most. Ask students why they answered the way they did. Ask what makes a good restaurant, and what makes a bad restaurant.
- Discuss as a class.

▶ **Workbook p. 141, Activities 1 and 2**

Lesson 6   Student's Book pp. 60 and 61

✔ **Homework Check!**

Workbook p. 141, Activities 1 and 2

Answers
1 Read the recipe quickly. Then circle the correct option.
1. fruit, 2. ingredients
2 Complete the shopping list for 12 cupakes.
1. 500 grams, 2. 4, 3. 2 ½ cups, 4. 2 teaspoons, 5. 1 cup

Warm-up

Students brainstorm the qualities of a good restaurant.
- Have students work in small groups to make a list of the characteristics of a good restaurant.
- After three minutes, ask one person from each group to share their ideas.
- Ask the class if they agree with each group. What does each group want in a good restaurant?

3 🎧¹⁸ **Listen and number the speakers.**

Students listen to the audio and write the numbers of the speakers next to two of the screen names.

Answers

Brianna2003 2, *AustinPeace* 1

Audio Script

1. BOY 1: So, how do you like this place?
   BOY 2: Uhmm, I don't like it very much…
   BOY 1: Why?
   BOY 2: Look at this burger! The bread is hard and the beef tastes awful!
   BOY 1: Come on! It's not so bad… The fries taste good.
   BOY 2: They're OK.
   SERVER: Hey, guys. Guess what? We don't have chocolate milkshake tonight.
   BOY 2: Grrr… Why do I still come here?
2. GIRL 1: So, how do you like this place?
   GIRL 2: Oh, I love it! The options on the menu are great.
   GIRL 1: And are the prices good?
   GIRL 2: Yes, they are! Look! The food is healthy, the fruits and vegetables are fresh…
   GIRL 1: Are you a vegetarian?
   GIRL 2: Me? No! But I like vegetarian restaurants, you know…
   SERVER: Good afternoon. Are you ready to order?

4 Categorize the words in a chart in your notebook: *positive* (+), *negative* (–) and *both* (+ –).

Students characterize words for qualities as positive, negative or both.

Answers

positive (+): great, good, delicious, awesome
negative (-): awful, gross, bad
both (+-): okay, cheap, expensive

5 Ask and answer with a classmate.

Students ask and answer questions about their opinions of a restaurant they know using the models.

Answers

Answers will vary.

Wrap-up

Repeat Activity 5, but have students ask about their favorite foods instead of restaurants.

➡ **Workbook p. 141, Activity 3**

Preparing for the Next Lesson
Ask students to watch an introduction to La Tomatina: goo.gl/jczGCW.

> 🐝 **Teaching Tip**
> **Monitoring During Speaking Activities**
> Circulating around the room during a speaking activity can help you check in on students' understanding. As you walk around, listen to what students are saying. Is there any grammar or vocabulary students need to review? This is a good way to use formative assessment in the classroom in an informal way.

 **Culture**

Objectives
Students will be able to explore a famous food festival and discuss whether it is OK to waste food.

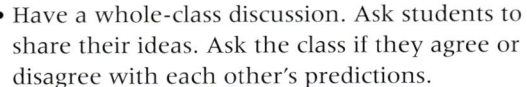 Student's Book pp. 62 and 63

✔ **Homework Check!**
Workbook p. 141, Activity 3
Answers
3 Think of your favorite recipe or dish. Write a shopping list for it in your notebook.
Answers will vary.

Warm-up
Students preview the culture reading and themes.
• Have students look at the photos.
• Ask *What do you see? What do you think La Tomatina is?*
• Have a whole-class discussion. Ask students to share their ideas. Ask the class if they agree or disagree with each other's predictions.

 64

1 Read the first paragraph and complete the sentences.
Students preview the text by reading the first paragraph and answering questions.
Answers
1. Bunol, 2. August, 3. tomatoes

2 Read the rest of the article and underline the answers in the article.
Students read the rest of the article and search for information.
Answers
1. around 20,000, 2. for one hour, 3. 1945

Extension
Students discuss the festival.
• In small groups, have students discuss their ideas.
• Ask *Would you participate in La Tomatina? Why or why not?*
• Circulate around the room as students discuss their answers. Listen to check their understanding of the article.
• After five minutes, bring the class together to share their ideas.

Wrap-up
Students play a timed game to answer extra questions about the article.
• Separate students into small groups.
• Have students race to answer all of the following questions about the article:
  1. How much does it cost to participate in La Tomatina?
  2. How many tomatoes are used in the food fight?
  3. How are the tomatoes transported to the event?
  4. Name two events that occur in preparation for La Tomatina.
  5. How do participants know when to stop and start throwing tomatoes?
• Have students raise their hands when they are done. Check their answers.
• The first group to answer all questions correctly wins.

Answers
1. 10 euros 2. 150,000, 3. Trucks bring the tomatoes. 4. There are events with music, dancing, food and fireworks. 5. When participants hear a loud sound, they stop and start throwing tomatoes.

▶ **(No homework today.)**

Lesson 8   Student's Book pp. 62 and 63

Warm-up
Students review and summarize the article on *La Tomatina*.
- Have students work in pairs.
- Assign one paragraph of the article to each student.
- Ask each student to summarize their paragraph to their partner.
- After a few minutes, bring the class together to share summaries.
- Ask the class to vote on the best summary for each paragraph. These will make up the whole-class summary of the article.

3 🎧¹⁹ **Listen and match. What are the visitors' opinions?**
Students listen to the audio and match the opinions to the speakers.

Answers
1. *Mia* It's fun!, 2. *Connor* It's a waste of good food.
3. *Chloe La Tomatina* can be a dangerous activity.

Audio Script
The *La Tomatina* festival has just finished. Our question is, "What do you think about the festival?"
1. Mia
Hi, I'm Mia. *La Tomatina* is great! It's a lot of fun to throw tomatoes. I want to do it again next year. I love it!
2. Connor
Hi, my name is Connor and I don't like this festival. It's a waste of food. You can eat all these tomatoes, but now they're just trash! They can have a tomato soup festival, and we can eat lots of tomato soup.
3. Chloe
My name is Chloe. I like *La Tomatina*, but there are too many people. It can be dangerous. I fell and hurt my arm. And look, I'm wearing new shoes and now they are destroyed. *La Tomatina* is fun, but you need to prepare for it.

4 🎧¹⁹ **Listen again and mark (✓) the ideas you hear.**
Students listen for details and mark the ideas they hear the speakers express.

Answers
3. You can fall and hurt your body. 4. You need to wear old clothes and sneakers.

Stop and Think! Critical Thinking
Is it OK to waste large amounts of food in festivals such as *La Tomatina*?
- Draw students' attention to the **Stop and Think!** box and read the question aloud.
- Have students discuss their ideas with a partner.
- After five minutes, ask the class to raise their hands if they think it is OK to waste large amounts of food in festivals. Then write the number of votes on the board. Then ask students to raise their hands if they think it is not OK to waste food in festivals. Write the number of votes on the board.
- Group students who answered for each side together. Ask each team to discuss their answer and give reasons in a class debate.
- Allow each team to share their opinions.

Wrap-up
Students briefly summarize the debate.
- Ask students to think of the main ideas that each side brought up in the debate.
- Write students' ideas in two lists (one for each side of the debate) on the board.
- Ask students if both sides agreed on anything. Write students' agreements on the board in a separate list.

➡ **(No homework today.)**

Teaching Tip
Conducting Debates
When asking students to debate, remind them that it's OK to disagree with each other. You can also tell them that in debates, we speak to each other respectfully.

 **Project**

Objective
Students will be able to plan a healthy menu.

Lesson 9   Student's Book p. 64

Warm-up

Tell students to look at the food pictures on page 64. Ask *Which foods look most delicious? Why?* Have students discuss their ideas with a partner.

1 Label the food and drink items in the tables. Use the words provided.

Students label the food and drink pictures.

Answers

A popcorn, orange juice, baked potato,
B chocolate cream cookies, apple pie, ice cream

2 Complete the Venn diagram. How are Table A and Table B similar and different?

 66

Students complete the Venn diagram showing similarities and differences between Table A and Table B.

Answers

Similar Both tables have food made from the same ingredients, like popcorn, apples and potatoes.
Different Foods in Table A are healthier (they are less processed and have less sugar and fat) than the foods in Table B.

Wrap-up

Students categorize food and drink in the unit as healthy or unhealthy.
- Go through the pages in the unit and point at different pictures of food (for example, on pages 56–58).
- For each photo, ask *Is it healthy or unhealthy?* Have students guess the answers and mark with a ✓ for healthy, and an ✗ for unhealthy.
- Have students compare answers with a partner.

Lesson 10 Student's Book p. 65

Warm-up
Students discuss healthy and unhealthy options in restaurants.
- Have a whole-class discussion. Ask students to think about the last time they went to a restaurant and ordered food. Ask *Was the food healthy or unhealthy? How about the time before? Was the food healthy or unhealthy? What are some healthy options we can find in local restaurants?*

3 Read the menu and circle the healthy options.
Students read the menu and decide which foods on the menu are healthy.
- Draw students' attention to the **Guess What!** box. Read the information aloud and ask why they think so many students in the US get free or reduced price lunches.

Answers
Lettuce and tomato salad

4 Work with a partner. Write a healthy menu.
Students work with a partner to create a healthy menu.
- Have students follow the instructions on the page.
- Point out to students that they can use the menu on page 65 as a model to set up their menu.

Answers
Answers will vary.

> **The Digital Touch**
> To incorporate digital media in the project, suggest the following:
> - Students can create their menus in Word or in Google Docs.
>
> Note that students should have the option to do a task on paper or digitally.

Wrap-up
Students vote on which menus show the following qualities the best: best design, healthiest food, most delicious food, most interesting food.
- Have students vote for each category. Ask students to write their answers on a piece of paper and fold it up. Collect the answers and tally them. Announce the winners at the beginning of the next class.

 **Workbook p. 140, Activity 1 (Review)**

> **Teaching Tip**
> **Displaying Student Work**
> Allowing students to display their work can be very encouraging and exciting for them. This can increase motivation, and students may produce higher quality work if they know they will have an audience.

Review

Objective
Students will be able to consolidate their understanding of the vocabulary and grammar learned in the unit.

Lesson 11   Student's Book p. 66

✔ **Homework Check!**
Workbook p. 140, Activity 1 (Review)

Answers
1 Look at the illustration and correct the sentences in your notebook.
1. ~~apple~~ There aren't any <u>apples</u>.
2. ~~any~~ We can see <u>some</u> tomatoes.
3. ~~some~~ We can't see <u>any</u> oranges.
4. ~~are~~ There <u>is</u> some broccoli.
5. ~~any~~ There is <u>some</u> garlic.

Warm-up
Students describe what they had for breakfast today.
- Have students work in pairs.
- Students write their partners' answers down and report them to the class.
- After students report answers, ask the class if anyone had similar breakfasts. Do we eat similar or different things for breakfast?

1 Unscramble the words.
Students unscramble the food and drink words.

Answers
1. beef, 2. milk, 3. cheese, 4. fish, 5. butter, 6. pasta

2 Complete the crossword.
Students do a crossword puzzle to review food and drink vocabulary.

Answers
Down 1. rice, 3. tomato, 4. water, 6. bread
Across 2. fish, 5. orange, 7. egg, 8. carrot

3 Organize the items from Activities 1 and 2. Then add two other items to each column.
Students organize the food and drink items from Activities 1 and 2 into the three categories according to their preferences.

Answers
Answers will vary.

Wrap-up
Students review food words by playing a game.
- Have students create a table in their notebooks with two columns and 17 rows:

Food	Name

- Write a list of food and drink words on the board for students to complete the first column of their tables: *apple, banana, beans, beef, bread, broccoli, butter, carrot, cheese, chicken, egg, fish, onions, oranges, pasta, rice.*
- Tell students to go around the classroom asking each other which of the foods they like, and writing a classmate's name by the food that he or she likes.
- Students race to complete their tables by finding someone who likes each food.

 (No homework today.)

Lesson 12 Student's Book p. 67

Warm-up

Students share their favorite recipes.

- Ask students to write down a recipe they know. This could be for their favorite dish.
- Give the recipe a title. The title could be the name of the food.
- Have students share their recipes in small groups.
- Ask students to list any ingredients which appear in more than one recipe. Which ingredients are most popular? Why?

4 Look at the underlined words. Write C (countable) or U (uncountable).

Students review countable and uncountable nouns by labeling words in sentences.

Answers

1. U, 2. C, 3. U, 4. C, 5. U, 6. U

5 Circle the correct option.

Students review *some* and *any* by choosing which word correctly completes each sentence.

Answers

1. some, 2. any, 3. any, 4. any, 5. some, 6. any

6 Look and write the missing ingredient.

Students look at the picture and write the missing ingredient in the recipe.

Answer

tomatoes

7 Mark (✓) the correct dish.

Students identify the dish that the recipe in Activity 6 makes.

Answer

Spaghetti bolognese

 Big Question

Students are given the opportunity to revisit the Big Question and reflect on it.

- Ask students to turn to the unit opener on page 55 and look at the question, "What do we eat?"
- Have students work in small groups. Ask them to discuss the question based on their work in this unit.
- Tell students to think about the things they eat for breakfast, lunch and dinner. Then tell them to think about the things they might eat in a restaurant. Ask *Are they the same? Are they different? Which do you like better? Which meal is healthiest for you?*

 Scorecard

Hand out (and/or project) a *Scorecard*. Have students fill in their *Scorecards* for this unit.

➡ **Study for the unit test.**

5 Why do we need a vacation?

Grammar	Vocabulary
Verb *be*: *was*, *were*: The art museum <u>was</u> open on Monday. In the past, it <u>wasn't</u> open on Mondays.	**Tourist Attractions:** amusement park, aquarium, art museum, beach, historic center, mountains, street market, zoo **Adjectives:** beautiful, boring, crowded, fun, great, noisy, terrible

Listening	Writing
Predicting the information	Making a vacation scrapbook

In the first lesson, read the unit title aloud and have students look carefully at the unit cover. Encourage them to think about the message in the picture. At the end of the unit, students will discuss the big question: *Why do we need a vacation?*

Teaching Tip
Allowing for Flexibility
Some students may not have much experience with vacations. To help these students feel more included, be sure to allow for some creativity and flexibility when talking about past vacations. Tell students that they can talk about made-up vacations, or imagine vacations they would like to take.

Vocabulary

Objectives
Students will be able to use **places** vocabulary and **adjectives** to talk about vacations.

Lesson 1
Student's Book p. 70

Warm-up
Students activate previous knowledge about vacations.
- Write the word *vacation* on the board and ask students *What is a vacation?*
- Elicit ideas from the class. Students share their descriptions (adjectives, ideas) of what a vacation is to them.

1 🎧 20 **Label the pictures. Then listen and check.**
Students practice places vocabulary by labeling photos with the vacation place each shows. Then students listen to the audio to check their answers.

Audio Script
Here are the top attractions in Bongo Beach:
Number 1 is the beach. It's the most popular attraction.
Number 2 is the aquarium.
Number 3 is the street market.
Number 4 is the art museum. It's not very popular.
Now let's look at the attractions in Triple Peaks:
The top attraction, number 1, is the mountains.
Number 2 is the historic center.
Number 3 is the zoo!
Number 4 is the amusement park. It's old and not very attractive.

2 Think Fast! List the attractions you can a) probably find in Hawaii, and b) visit in your town or city.
Students do a three-minute timed challenge: they write a list of the attractions they can probably find in Hawaii and the attractions they can visit in their town or city.

Answers
Answers will vary.

Extension
Students identify famous tourist attractions in their country.
- Students form small groups.
- Ask *What are three famous tourist attractions in this country? Name them and say what kind of place they are.*
- Tell students to discuss and list the three attractions with the kind of place each is (e.g. *art museum, beach*).
- After 5 – 10 minutes, elicit ideas from the class.
- List the attractions each group names on the board.

Wrap-up
Students review places vocabulary for tourist attractions by playing a game.
- Tell students what you "see" in a certain location: *I see paintings, sculptures and drawings.*
- Students guess where you are. (Answer: an art museum)
- Repeat for *amusement park, aquarium, beach, historic center, mountains, street market* and *zoo*.

⏵ **Workbook p. 142, Activity 1**

Lesson 2 — Student's Book p. 71

> ✔ **Homework Check!**
> Workbook p. 142, Activity 1
> **Answers**
> **1 Write the names of the tourist attractions.**
> 1. zoo, 2. art museum, 3. aquarium, 4. street market,
> 5. mountain, 6. historic center, 7. beach

Warm-up
Students review places vocabulary for tourist attractions.
- Write the following words on the board: *beach, mountains, zoo, aquarium, amusement park.*
- Assign volunteers to draw each word on the board without letting the class hear which word each student will draw.
- When students have finished drawing, ask the class which word each drawing illustrates.

3 Think Fast! Look at the information and identify the best attractions of Bongo Beach.
Students do a one-minute timed challenge: they quickly read the information about Bongo Beach and identify the best attractions. Ask students *How can you tell which attractions are the best?* Elicit *The best ones have more stars.*

Answers
Mango Beach, the Bongo Aquarium

4 Read the information. Then read and match.
Students read the information about Bongo Beach and match adjective phrases used in the text with their meanings.

Answers
top to bottom 4, 3, 1, 5, 6, 2, 7

Stop and Think! Critical Thinking
What do you prefer for a vacation, the beach or the mountains? Why?
- Students form small groups to discuss what they can do on vacation at the beach and what they can do on vacation in the mountains.
- Encourage students to make Pro / Con lists of beach and mountain vacations to decide which they prefer. (Pro = good things about it, Con = bad things about it.)
- Invite a presenter for each group to share the group's preference and reasons with the class.

Wrap-up
Students practice using adjectives to describe places.
- Tell students to describe the tourist attractions in the brochures on page 70. *What kinds of adjectives can describe them?*
- Students may use the descriptions in Activity 4 as a model.
- Encourage volunteers to share their answers with the class.

➡ **Workbook pp. 142 and 143, Activities 2 and 3**

Grammar

Objective
Students will be able to use the **verb *be* in past** to talk about past vacations.

Lesson 3 — Student's Book pp. 72 and 73

✔ **Homework Check!**
Workbook pp. 142 and 143, Activities 2 and 3

Answers
2 Write adjectives from the unit using the letters in the box. Then answer.
1. great, 2, fun, 3. noisy, 4. terrible,
5. beautiful; crowded
3 Match the comments.
top to bottom 1, 0, 4, 3, 2, 5

Warm-up
Students review vocabulary for vacation places by completing sentences.
- Write the following sentences on the board with gaps for students to fill:
  » I swim at the _____.
  » I ride roller coasters at the _____.
  » I see fish at the _____.
  » I see elephants and lions at the _____.
- Have students complete the sentences and check answers as a class.

Answers
beach, amusement park, aquarium, zoo

1 🎧²¹ Listen to the comic story.
Have students listen to the comic story and follow along with the pictures on page 72. Play the audio twice. Then ask *Where did the girl go?* Elicit answers from the class.

Audio Script
1. GIRL: Hey, Dan, do you want to see some vacation pictures?
   BOY: Sure, Ann!
2. BOY: Wow! You look scared! Were you in Egypt?
   GIRL: Yes, and I was really afraid.
3. BOY: Were you in Paris with your parents?
   GIRL: Yes, we were, but I wasn't in this picture. I was in another, uh, place.
4. BOY: Wow, were you with the British Royal Family?
   GIRL: Yes, I was… They weren't very active.
5. BOY: And where were you here?
   GIRL: I was at an amusement park in the US. I was all wet after a water ride.
6. BOY: That's fantastic! You were in Egypt, France, the UK and the US!
   GIRL: Not really! We were at the Round the World Park in Florida!
   BOY: Oh, I thought you were really on a trip around the world!

2 🎧²¹ Number the dialogues of the story. Then listen again and check.
Students number the dialogues of the story to match the order they occur in the audio.

Answers
left to right, top to bottom 2, 4, 6, 5, 1, 3

Extension
Students rate the attractions in the comic.
- Students form small groups.
- Tell the groups to rate the attractions in the comic from five stars (best) to one star (worst).
- Ask each group to share their star ratings and write them on the board.
- Ask the class *Do you agree or disagree? Why?* Discuss as a class.

Wrap-up
Students discuss the comic in more detail.
- Ask students questions about the comic to invite students to discuss what was happening in each scene: *Why do you think Ann was afraid in Egypt? Why does she say the British Royal Family wasn't very active? Did Ann enjoy the water ride?*

➡ **Workbook p. 143, Activity 1**

🐝 **Teaching Tip**
Organizing Group Work Tasks
When asking students to do group work, have students assign roles for themselves. For example, there could be a note taker or a presenter. The note taker should take notes on the group's conversation and decisions. The presenter will share the group's notes and ideas with the class.

Lesson 4   Student's Book pp. 72 and 73

> ✔ Homework Check!
> Workbook p. 143, Activity 1
> **Answers**
> **1 Complete the sentences using *was* or *were*.**
> 1. was, 2. were, 3. was, 4. were, 5. was, 6. was

Warm-up

Students review the comic story using the verb *be* in past.
- Tell students to turn to p. 72 in their books.
- Ask *Where did the girl go? What did she see?*
- Invite student volunteers to describe what happened in each comic picture: *Ann was on a camel. Ann was afraid.*

3 Circle the correct verbs.

Students choose the correct form of the verb *be* in past to complete the sentences.
- Draw students' attention to the **Present → Past** box and read the information aloud.

Answers
1. were, 2. wasn't, 3. were, 4. weren't, 5. was, 6. were

4 Match the questions to the answers.

Students match the questions about the comic to the answers.

Answers
top to bottom 5, 4, 2, 1, 3

5 Think Fast! In your notebook, write two more questions about the comic using *was* and *were*.

Students do a two-minute timed challenge: they write two questions about the comic using *was* and *were*.
- Tell students that they can use the questions in Activity 4 as a model.
- After two minutes, ask volunteers to write their questions on the board.
- Correct the questions as necessary and ask the class if they can answer the questions.

Wrap-up

Students correct sentences to review the forms of the verb *be* in past.
- Write the following sentences on the board and ask students to correct them. The first student to correct all the sentences wins.
  » *I weren't in Mexico last week.*
  » *Ann were on vacation in May.*
  » *Joe and Tina wasn't at school yesterday.*

Answers
wasn't, was, weren't

▶ **Workbook p. 144, Activities 2–4**

Objectives
Students will be able to identify specific information in an audio clip. They will also be able to use **places** vocabulary, **adjectives** and the **verb be in past** to create a vacation scrapbook.

Lesson 5 Student's Book pp. 74 and 75

> ✔ **Homework Check!**
> Workbook pp. 143 and 144, Activities 2–4
> **Answers**
> **2 Mark the sentences correct (✔) or incorrect (✘). Rewrite the incorrect sentences.**
> 1. (✔), 2. (✘) ~~wasn't~~ Mel and Julia weren't at the beach on Saturday., 3. (✘) ~~wasn't~~ We weren't at the street market on Monday., 4. (✘) ~~was~~ The tourists were interested in the art museum., 5. (✘) ~~Were~~ Was Alex at the zoo on Tuesday?, 6. (✔)
> **3 Rewrite the sentences using the information in parentheses.**
> 1. The old art museum wasn't on Baker Street.
> 2. The beach wasn't polluted last year.
> 3. The tigers at the City Zoo were hungry.
> 4. Was Alyssa interested in the historic center?
> 5. The tourists were happy at the street market.
> **4 In your notebook, write sentences using information from the table.**
> 1. In the past, it was terrible.
> 2. In the past, they were polluted.
> 3. In the past, it was bad for kids.
> 4. In the past, it was not a tourist attraction.

Warm-up
Students review the verb *be* in past by completing sentences.
- Write the following sentences on the board with gaps for students to fill: 1. Jessica _____ in China last year. (+) 2. Darren _____ in Egypt last month. (-) 3. Maria and Ann _____ in London last week. (+) 4. They _____ in Scotland. (-)

Answers
was, wasn't, were, weren't

1 Think Fast! List the countries in the scrapbook.
Students do a one-minute timed challenge: they list all the countries included in the scrapbook.

Answers
China, Egypt, Australia

2 🎧²² Listen to Isabella's presentation and confirm your answers.
Students listen to an audio presentation of a vacation and follow along with the photos in the scrapbook. They listen for names of countries to check their answers to Activity 1.

Audio Script
In the second part of my trip, I was in three countries. First stop: Egypt—a very interesting country. The street markets were so noisy! Look at the picture of Cairo in my scrapbook: can you see the pyramids in the background?
The plan was to go to Thailand, but there was no time.
So then, China! The places were beautiful. The only problem in China was eating insects: they were terrible! Yuck!
And finally, Australia. I was at the beaches—Bondi Beach was great! My two little sisters were with kangaroos at the Sydney Zoo. The zoo was really fun!

3 🎧²² Read the sentences and predict the words. Then listen and complete the sentences.
Students preview the sentences in the Activity to predict words they will hear when they listen to the audio again. They complete the sentences with adjectives and one noun from the audio.
- Draw students' attention to the **Be Strategic!** box and read the information aloud.

Answers
1. interesting, 2. noisy, 3. beautiful, 4. terrible, 5. great, 6. sisters

Wrap-up
Students discuss the countries included in the trip presentation.
- Write *China*, *Egypt* and *Australia* on the board and tell students to vote for the country they would like to visit most.
- Tally students' votes and ask *Why did you vote for China / Australia / Egypt?* Elicit ideas from students.

➡ **Workbook p. 145, Activity 1**

💭 Teaching Tip
Managing Fast Finishers
Some students complete activities more quickly than others, so it's a good idea to have a few extra activities on hand, otherwise these students may become bored and disruptive. One set of activities designed for fast finishers are the *Just for Fun* pages. Students can work on these individually and then check their answers in the back of the Student's Book. The *Just for Fun* activities for this unit are on page 82.

Lesson 6   Student's Book pp. 74 and 75

> ✔ **Homework Check!**
> Workbook p. 145, Activity 1
> **Answers**
> **1 Read the blog post and number the pictures.**
> *top to bottom* 2, 5, 4, 3, 1

Warm-up
Students describe the places in the scrapbook on pages 74 and 75 using adjectives.
- Write each country name on the board (*China, Australia, Egypt*) and tell students to describe each country using adjectives and the information in the scrapbook.
- As students share adjectives, write them next to each country and ask the class if they agree or disagree.

4 Circle the correct words.
Students choose the correct words to complete sentences about scrapbooks.

Answers
1. personal, 2. special moments, 3. pictures

5 Now write a page for a vacation scrapbook—print or digital. Follow the steps below.
Students create a scrapbook page for a real or imaginary vacation.

Wrap-up
Students ask each other about their scrapbook pages using the verb *be* in past.
- Have students think of questions using the verb *be* in past that they could ask each other about the vacation scrapbook pages they made in Activity 5.
- Provide some example questions: *Was the country beautiful? Was the historic center noisy?*
- Give students a few minutes to write questions, then tell students to walk around the room and ask and answer questions with their classmates.

➡ **Workbook p. 145, Activity 2**

Preparing for the Next Lesson
Ask students to watch an introduction to Mardi Gras from National Geographic: goo.gl/mX8GLJ or invite them to look around on the History channel web site: goo.gl/Yysard.

 **Teaching Tip**
Guiding Students
If students have trouble thinking of real or imaginary places to describe in their scrapbooks, give them some suggestions. They could describe a trip to some of the places they have learned about in other units: London, Spain, Japan, etc.

 **Culture**

Objective
Students will be able to appreciate the role of festivals and celebrations in culture by learning about an example: Mardi Gras in the US.

Lesson 7   Student's Book pp. 76 and 77

> ✔ **Homework Check!**
> Workbook p. 145, Activity 2
>
> **Answers**
> 2 Write a blog post about a tourist attraction using *was* and *were*.
> Answers will vary.

Warm-up
Students preview the article by looking at the pictures on pages 76 and 77.
- Ask *What do you see in the pictures? What is Mardi Gras?* Elicit answers from the class.

1 Read the article about Mardi Gras and number the parts.
Students read the article independently and match the parts with the paragraph each describes.
- Draw students' attention to the **Guess What!** box on page 76 and read the information aloud.

Answers
left to right 2, 1, 3

2 Think Fast! Look and identify: a ball, a float, jazz musicians, a King cake.
Students do a one-minute timed challenge: they label the pictures at the top of page 77 with *a ball, a float, jazz musicians* or *a King cake*.

Wrap-up
Ask the class if they would like to attend Mardi Gras one day. Ask *Why do you / don't you want to go?* Elicit ideas from students.

➡ **(No homework today.)**

Lesson 8   Student Book pp. 76 and 77

Warm-up

Students review the main ideas of the article on Mardi Gras.
- Ask *What was the article about?*
- Guide students to look at the first sentences of each paragraph to find the main ideas: *Mardi Gras is the celebration of Carnival in New Orleans. Nowadays, over a million people enjoy Mardi Gras in New Orleans. The traditional food of Mardi Gras is the King cake–a cake with a small plastic baby inside.* Elicit ideas from the class.

3 Circle T (True) or F (False).

Students read the statements about Mardi Gras and choose whether each is true or false based on the information in the article.

Answers

1. F (Its origin is in the French language.), 2. T, 3. F (Over a million people enjoy Mardi Gras in New Orleans.), 4. T, 5. F (People look for a small plastic doll inside the King Cake.)

4 Look and number the descriptions of the Mardi Gras words.

Students match the words filled in on the crossword puzzle with the clues to the right.

Answers

top to bottom 5, 7, 1, 6, 8, 3, 4, 2

Stop and Think! Critical Thinking

Do people travel to attend festivals or celebrations in your country?
- Have students list some festivals or celebrations in their country and where the festivals occur.
- Ask students *Do people travel to attend any of these festivals? Have you ever traveled to attend a festival?*
- If time permits, ask students what things about a festival might make people want to travel to attend it.

Wrap-up

Have students review adjectives and use them to describe Mardi Gras.
- Write the following words on the board: *beautiful, boring, crowded, fun, great, interesting, noisy, terrible.*
- Ask volunteers to cross out words which don't describe Mardi Gras. Ask the class if they agree or disagree and why.

⏩ **(No homework today.)**

 **Project**

> **Objective**
> Students will be able to make a podcast about a vacation destination.

Lesson 9   Student's Book pp. 78 and 79

Warm-up

Students review vocabulary for places by playing a game of Hangman. Then ask students to give an example of each word in real life. For example, a real beach, a real amusement park, etc.

1  **Listen to the podcast and complete the information.**

Students read the information in the graphic organizer and in the word box; then they listen to the podcast and complete the information in the mind map.

Answers

1. Caribbean, 2. Old, fortresses, 3. beaches, Park, 4. hotels

Audio Script

Hi! My name's Trevor and this is The Teen Travel Podcast. Today I'm going to talk about San Juan, Puerto Rico!
1. San Juan is the capital of Puerto Rico, an island in the Caribbean.
2. The city is famous for its beaches and for its amazing historic center, known as Old San Juan. In Old San Juan, you can visit two fortresses: El Morro and Castillo San Cristóbal.
3. The best beach in San Juan is Isla Verde, but people also like Ocean Park a lot.
4. And in terms of accommodation, where can you stay? The best hotels are on the beach, but you can also stay in Old San Juan.

2 Create a podcast about a vacation destination.

Students follow the steps to develop a podcast. They complete the mind map to organize their ideas.

3 Write an outline for your podcast using the diagram.

Groups outline their podcasts following the steps in the diagram.

Wrap-up

Groups share the places they chose to describe in their podcasts with the class. Invite each group to share and to tell why they chose that place.

Teaching Tip

Giving Instructions

When doing group work, split students into their groups before giving instructions for an activity. Students will be less distracted once they are settled into their groups and will understand the instructions much more easily.

Lesson 10
Student Book pp. 78 and 79

Warm-up
Students review adjectives from the unit by playing a game of Charades.
- Secretly ask a student to act out a word (*beautiful, boring, crowded, fun, great, interesting, noisy, terrible*). The first student to guess the word wins, and the winner acts out the next word.

4 In your group, use the outline to write a script for your podcast.

Students write the scripts for their podcasts following the instructions given.
- Ask students to get into their groups from Lesson 9 and to review their mind maps and diagrams from Activities 2 and 3.
- Read the steps in Activity 4 aloud and have students follow along.
- Then have groups begin writing the scripts for their podcasts.

5 Record your podcast using a cell phone, tablet or computer. Then share it with your class.

Students record their podcasts and present them to the class.

Stop and Think! Critical Thinking
After listening to the podcasts, which vacation destination would you like to visit? Why?
- List the vacation destinations students discussed in their podcasts on the board.
- Tell students to give two details about each vacation destination to note on the board.
- Then have students vote for the destination they would most like to visit and tally their votes on the board.
- Ask students *Which destination did you vote for? Why is it your favorite?*

The Digital Touch
To incorporate digital media in the project, suggest one or more of the following:
- Students record their podcasts using a cell phone, tablet or computer.
- Students find photos on the Internet of their vacation destination to accompany the recording of their podcast.

Note that students should have the option to do a task on paper or digitally.

Wrap-up
Students discuss the two or three vacation destinations that were the most popular.
- Ask students *Which two (or three) vacation destinations got the most votes?* Write stars by those destinations on the board.
- Then ask *What is the location of each destination?* and *What attractions does each destination have?* Note the answers under each destination.
- Then ask *What adjectives could you use to describe each destination?* Note the answers on the board.
- Finally, ask *What do the most popular vacation destinations have in common?* Elicit ideas from the class.

▶ **Workbook p. 144, Activity 1 (Review)**

Review

Objective
Students will be able to consolidate their understanding of the vocabulary and grammar they have learned in the unit.

Lesson 11 Student's Book p. 80

✔ **Homework Check!**
Workbook p. 144, Activity 1 (Review)
Answers
1 In your notebook, answer the questions.
Answers will vary.

Warm-up
Students review vocabulary for tourist attractions in a personalization activity. Ask students *Where did you go on vacation? What tourist attractions did you go to?* Elicit ideas from the class.

1 Label the places.
Students complete the sentences to label the photos of vacation places.
Answers
left to right, top to bottom art museum, historic center, zoo, beach, mountain, amusement park, aquarium, street market

2 Mark (✔) the correct adjectives.
Students mark the adjective that best completes each sentence.
Answers
1. crowded, 2. boring, 3. terrible, 4. noisy, 5. fun

3 Complete the description words with vowels.
Students fill in the blanks to complete the adjectives.
Answers
1. beautiful, 2. boring, 3. crowded, 4. fun, 5. great, 6. interesting, 7. noisy, 8. terrible

Extension
Students practice adjectives by using them in sentences.
- Have students write a sentence in their notebooks describing something with each description word in Activity 3.
- Tell students to exchange their sentences with a partner and edit each other's sentences.
- Elicit sample sentences from the class.

Wrap-up
Students practice using adjectives to describe destinations explored in the unit.
- Write the words *China, Australia, Egypt* and *New Orleans* on the board.
- Have students work in small groups. Tell them to describe these places using adjectives they learned in the unit.

▶ **(No homework today.)**

Lesson 12 Student's Book p. 81

Warm-up

Students write sentences to review the verb *be* in past.
- Write *was, were, wasn't* and *weren't* on the board.
- Have students write a sentence using each word correctly in their notebooks.
- Have students exchange notebooks and check their sentences.

4 Look at the table. Then complete the sentences with *was, were, wasn't* or *weren't*.

Students use the information in the table to complete the sentences with *was, were, wasn't* or *weren't*.

Answers

1. weren't, 2. was, 3. were, 4. was, 5. was

5 Complete the conversation.

Students complete the conversation about the information in Activity 4 with the correct forms of the verb *be* in past.

Answers

1. were, 2. were, 3. were, 4. were, 5. was, 6. was, 7. was, 8. Was, 9. was, 10. Were, 11. weren't, 12. were

 Big Question

Students are given the opportunity to revisit the Big Question and reflect on it.
- Ask students to turn to the unit opener on page 69 and look at the question, *Why do we need a vacation?*
- Have students work in small groups. Ask them to discuss the question based on their work in this unit.
- Tell students to think about the places and attractions they have read about this unit and the podcasts they made in Lesson 10.
- Ask students to think about why people go on vacations and the role vacation plays in people's lives.

Scorecard

Hand out (and/or project) a *Scorecard*. Have students fill in their *Scorecards* for this unit.

▶ Study for the unit test.

6 What's your story?

Grammar
Past simple: He first <u>met</u> his wife Consuelo in Buenos Aires in 1930.

Vocabulary
Movie and Book Genres: autobiography, children's books, fantasy, romance, action, animated, comedy, science fiction

Adjectives: boring, funny, sad, interesting, inspirational

Irregular Verbs: found, made, met, saw, went, wrote

Listening
Identifying sequence in a narrative

Writing
Connecting ideas in a past-tense text

What's your story?

In the first lesson, read the unit title aloud and have students look carefully at the unit cover. Encourage them to think about the message in the picture. At the end of the unit, students will discuss the big question: *What's your story?*

Teaching Tip
Embracing Differences
This is a good opportunity to remind students that the differences they may have with others can help to open their minds to new ideas, cultures and ways of doing things. Embracing differences can help students grow.

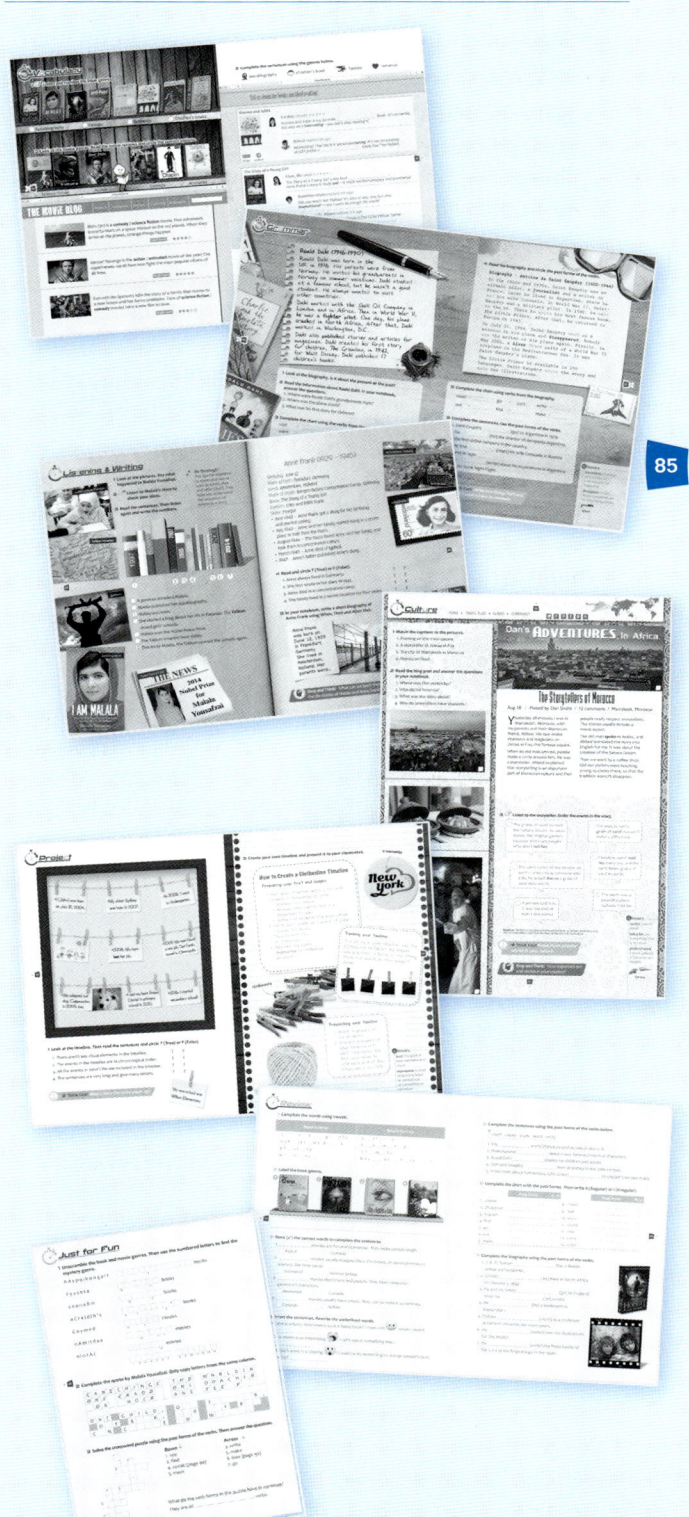

 **Vocabulary**

Objective
Students will be able to use genres and **adjectives** to talk about **books and movies**.

Lesson 1
Student's Book page 84

Warm-up
Students preview the unit and the unit question, *What's your story?*
- Have students work in small groups.
- Ask students to look through the pages in the unit.
- Ask *What's your story?*
- Have students write down the names of the people they will learn about in this unit. Tell students that these texts are called *biographies*. Elicit answers from the class.

Answers

Roald Dahl, Antoine de Saint Exupéry, Malala Yousafzai, Anne Frank

1 🎧²⁴ **Listen and number the book genres.**
Students learn books and movies vocabulary by listening to an audio.

Answers

left to right 3, 1, 2, 4

 86

Audio Script

1
GIRL 1: What's your favorite book genre?
BOY 1: Hmm… I really like fantasy books! I love *The Hobbit*! Those adventures in Middle Earth are awesome!
2
GIRL 1: I love romance books, and *Romeo and Juliet* is my favorite! It's not only about love. It has a lot of action, too!
3
GIRL 2: Do you like autobiographies?
GIRL 3: Yes, I do! *I am Malala* is one of the best books I've read!
4
BOY 1: What are you reading?
BOY 2: I'm reading *The Little Prince*.
BOY 1: Hey, that's a children's book!
BOY 2: Well, it's also for teens and adults.

2 Look at the movie genres. Read the movie reviews and circle the correct options.
Students are introduced to books and movies vocabulary by reading movie reviews.

Answers

top to bottom science fiction, action, comedy

Extension
Students explore genres.
- Have students work in small groups.
- Have each group write a description of the pictures at the bottom of page 84 in the movie reviews.
- Ask students what makes these pictures science fiction, action or comedy. What are the characteristics of these genres?
- Elicit answers from each group.

Wrap-up
Students review vocabulary for books and movies in a class conversation.
- Write the words for books and movies from page 84 on the board.
- Ask students to vote on their favorite genre. Each student may only vote once. Write the number of votes next to each word.
- Ask students which genre is the most popular in the class. Ask students what they like about that genre.

➡ **Workbook p. 146, Activities 1 and 2**

Lesson 2 — Student's Book p. 85

✔ **Homework Check!**
Workbook page 146, Activities 1 and 2

Answers

1 Label the movie and book genres.
1. comedy, 2. action, 3. science fiction,
4. autobiography, 5. romance, 6. children's book,
7. fantasy

2 Match the sentences.
top to bottom 1, 0, 2, 4, 6, 3, 5

Warm-up
Students review vocabulary by describing their favorite books and movies.
- Ask students to name some of their favorite movies and books. Ask students what their favorite autobiography, science fiction, action, comedy, romance and animated movies are. Then ask what their favorite children's books are.
- Elicit answers from students. Ask them what makes these books and movies a part of these genres.

3 Complete the sentences using the genres below.
Students practice using vocabulary for books and movies by completing sentences.

Answers

top to bottom romance, fantasy, autobiography, children's book

4 🎧²⁵ Listen and number the adjectives.
Students listen to the audio and number the adjectives that describe each book.

Answers

top to bottom 5, 4, 3, 2, 1

Audio Script
1. I liked reading *The Diary of a Young Girl*. The story is very inspirational. Anne Frank was a brave girl!
2. I watched *Mars 2312* with my little brother yesterday. It's so interesting we couldn't take our eyes off the TV screen.
3. I read *Romeo and Juliet* and I liked it. It's romantic, but it's also a historical novel. It's a sad story, though.
4. I liked *Fun with the Spencers*. It's a funny movie. Tom Lewis is one of my favorite comedy actors.
5. I didn't like *The Little Prince*. All that stuff about a prince and his rose is just… boring, you know!

5 Think Fast! In your notebook, write a movie or book title for each genre.
Students do a two-minute timed challenge: they quickly write a movie or book title for each genre.

Warm-up
Students review vocabulary for books and movies by playing a game of Hangman.
- Use books and movies vocabulary words from pages 84 and 85. When students complete a word, ask them to name an example for each genre.

➡ **Workbook p. 147, Activity 3**

💭 Teaching Tip
Engaging Students
Talking about students' favorite books and movies can bring a lot more energy to the classroom. Teenagers often love to share their opinions on popular culture. They might become more motivated to participate when they share their ideas about the things they enjoy.

 Grammar

Objective
Students will be able to use the **past simple of regular and irregular verbs** to talk about biographies and autobiographies.

Lesson 3
Student's Book p. 86

✔ Homework Check!
Workbook page 147, Activity 3

Answers
3 Complete the sentences using the adjectives.
1. Boring, 2. Interesting, 3. Sad, 4. Funny

Warm-up
Students review the definitions of *biography* and *autobiography*.
- Write the words *biography* and *autobiography* on the board.
- Ask students if they have ever read a biography or autobiography before.
- Ask a volunteer to give a definition for each. (Answer: Biography–a true story about someone's life; Autobiography–a story a person wrote about his or her own life.)
- Elicit examples of each from students.

 88

1 Look at the biography. Is it about the present or the past?
Students preview past simple verb forms by looking at the verbs in the biography.

Answer
past

2 Read the information about Roald Dahl. In your notebook, answer the questions.
Students read the biography and answer comprehension questions.

Answers
1. Norway, 2. North Africa, 3. *The Gremlins*

3 Complete the chart using the verbs from the article.
Students practice forming past simple verbs by completing a chart.
- Note that we change the final *-y* in *study* to *-ied* and we add *-d* to *create*.

Answers
left to right, top to bottom visited, studied, wanted, worked, crashed, published, created

Wrap-up
Students review past simple verb forms by playing a game.
- Have students close their books and notebooks.
- Separate students into small groups.
- Write a verb from page 86 on the board.
- Have groups race to give the past simple form of the verb and use it in a sentence. The first group to correctly give the past tense form and a sentence using the past tense verb gets a point. The group with the most points wins.

➡ **Workbook p. 147, Activities 1 and 2**

Lesson 4 Student's Book p. 87

> ✔ **Homework Check!**
> Workbook page 147, Activities 1 and 2
>
> **Answers**
> **1 Categorize the verbs.**
> *Verb* start, started; work, worked; *Verb ending in e* like, liked; love, loved; *Verb ending in vowel + y* play, played; *Verb ending in consonant + y* cry, cried; study, studied
> **2 Read and circle the correct verbs.**
> created, wanted, cried, asked, publish

Warm-up

Students review past simple verb forms on the board.

- Write the following sentences on the board with gaps for students to fill:
  Tara _____ (visit) her friends in California.
  Eric _____ (study) all night long.
  Jessica _____ (create) a story for her project.
- Elicit answers from students. Remind students that we usually add -ed to verbs to form the past tense. We change the final -y in *study* to –ied. We add –d to *create*.

4 Read the biography and circle the past forms of the verbs.

Students preview irregular past simple forms by looking at the verbs in the biography.

Answers

was, lived, met, was, went, wrote, returned, went, disappeared, saw, found, was, wrote, made

5 Complete the chart using verbs from the biography.

Students practice forming irregular past simple verbs by completing a chart.

Answers

met, *went*, wrote, saw, found, made

6 Complete the sentences. Use the past forms of the verbs.

Students practice using irregular past simple verb forms by completing sentences.

Answers

1. went, 2. was, 3. met, 4. wrote

7 Think Fast! Write two things Dahl and Saint-Exupéry have in common.

Students do a one-minute timed challenge: they quickly write two things Dahl and Saint-Exupéry have in common in their notebooks.

> **Extension**
> Students write for two minutes about Dahl and Saint-Exupéry's differences. Encourage students to use verbs in past simple form.
> - After two minutes, have students share their answers with a new partner. Ask students if they wrote the same or different things.
> - Bring the class back together for a class discussion. Elicit answers from students about Dahl and Saint-Exupéry's differences.
> - List students' ideas on the board.
> - Ask students if Dahl and Saint-Exupéry were more similar or more different from each other.

Wrap-up

Students review irregular past simple verb forms by playing a game.

- Have students close their books and notebooks. Erase the board.
- Separate students into small groups.
- Write the base forms of verbs on the board: *meet, go, see, write, find, make, disappear, crash, publish*.
- Have students race to give the irregular simple past form and a sentence correctly using the past verb.
- The first group to give the correct form and a correct sentence gets a point for each verb. The group with the most points wins.

➤ **Workbook p. 148, Activities 3 and 4**

Listening & Writing

Objectives
Students will be able to identify sequence in a narrative. They will also be able to connect ideas in a past-tense text.

Lesson 5 — Student's Book p. 88

✔ **Homework Check!**
Workbook page 148, Activities 3 and 4

Answers
3 Circle the irregular verbs and write them in the table.
make, made; meet, met; see, saw; write, wrote
4 Complete the sentences using past simple. Then circle T (True) or F (False).
1. met, F (Dahl and Saint-Exupéry were not friends.), 2. lived, T, 3. went, F (Saint-Exupéry went on a mission in his plane and disappeared.), 4. created, T, 5. wrote, F (*The Little Prince* is available in 250 languages.)

Warm-up
Students review irregular past simple verbs.
- Write the following sentences on the board with gaps for students to fill:
  Jen _____ (meet) her husband in New York.
  Thomas _____ (see) some famous actors in Los Angeles.
  Karen _____ (write) an autobiography for her class.
- Elicit answers from students: *met, saw, wrote*.

1 Look at the pictures. Say what happened to Malala Yousafzai.
Students preview the listening by looking at the pictures and making predictions.

2  **Listen to Malala's story to check your ideas.**
Students check their predictions by listening to the audio.
- Draw students' attention to the *Be Strategic!* box and read the information aloud. Encourage students to listen for dates.
- Ask students what information they got right. Ask *What clues helped you predict what happened to Malala?* Elicit answers from the class.

Audio Script
1. Malala Yousafzai was born in Pakistan in 1997.
2. When Malala was 10 years old, in 2007, the Taliban invaded the Swat Valley where she lived. Life was very difficult for girls in Pakistan.
3. In 2008, Malala started a blog about her life. When the Taliban closed all girls' schools, Malala wrote about girls' rights to education.
4. In 2009, the Taliban allowed Pakistani girls to study again.
5. On October 9, 2012, a Taliban gunman shot Malala. She recovered in a hospital in the UK.
6. In 2013, Malala published her autobiography.
7. Then, in 2014, she won the Nobel Peace Prize.

3 Read the sentences. Then listen again and write the numbers.
Students put the events of Malala's story in time order.

Answers
top to bottom 5, 6, 1, 3, 7, 2, 4

Wrap-up
Students review past simple verb forms by playing Hangman.
- Use common regular and irregular verbs in past simple from pages 86 and 87.
- When students complete a word, ask them to give a full sentence using the past simple form of the verb.

➡ **Workbook page 149, Activities 1 and 2**

> 💭 **Teaching Tip**
> **Managing Fast Finishers**
> Some students complete activities more quickly than others, so it's a good idea to have a few extra activities on hand, otherwise these students may become bored and disruptive. One set of activities designed for fast finishers are the *Just for Fun* pages. Students can work on these individually and then check their answers in the back of the Student's Book. The *Just for Fun* activities for this unit are on page 96.

Lesson 6   Student's Book p. 89

> ✔ **Homework Check!**
> Workbook page 149, Activities 1 and 2
> **Answers**
> **1 Complete the sentences with *When* or *After that*.**
> 1. When, 2. After that, 3. When
> **2 In your notebook, write about Edgar Allan Poe. Also use *Then*.**
> Answers will vary.

Warm-up
Students preview the pictures in Anne Frank's story.
- Have students look at the pictures on the page. Ask students *What do you think happened to Anne Frank?* Students should not read the biography yet.
- Elicit answers from the class.

4 Read and circle *T* (True) or *F* (False).
Students read the information about Anne Frank and determine whether statements are true or false.

Answers
1. F (She also lived in Amsterdam, Holland.), 2. T, 3. T, 4. F (The family lived in a secret location for two years.)

5 In your notebook, write a short biography of Anne Frank using *When, Then* and *After that*.
Students practice using *when, then* and *after that* for narrative sequence by writing a short biography of Anne Frank.

Stop and Think! Critical Thinking
What can we learn from the life stories of Malala and Anne Frank?
- Students discuss their ideas in small groups.
- Tell groups to list three to four things we can learn from each life story.
- After five minutes, bring the class together to discuss the question. List common responses on the board.

Wrap-up
Have students think of three to four events in their own lives and add them to a timeline on a sheet of paper. Then ask students to write a paragraph describing the events in their timelines in time order, using *When, Then* and *After that*. Ask volunteers to share their writing.

▶ **(No homework today.)**

Preparing for the Next Lesson
Ask students to watch an introduction to storytelling in Morocco: goo.gl/YGk6HA or invite them to read a magazine article about storytellers on the web site: goo.gl/o8kfmL.

 Culture

> **Objective**
> Students will be able to appreciate how oral storytelling passes culture down from one generation to the next.

Lesson 7   Student's Book pp. 90 and 91

Warm-up

Students preview the culture reading and themes on pages 90 and 91.
- Have students look at the photos on pages 90 and 91.
- Ask *What do you see? What country is this about?*
- Have students share their predictions in pairs.
- Have a whole-class discussion. Ask students to share their ideas.

1 Match the captions to the pictures.

Students label the photos on pages 90 and 91 with the correct captions.

Answers

top to bottom 3, 1, 4, 2

 2 Read the blog post and answer the questions in your notebook.

Students read the blog post and answer questions about it.

Answers

1. in Marrakesh, Morocco, 2. a storyteller, 3. the creation of the Sahara Desert, 4. so that the tradition doesn't disappear

Wrap-up

Students summarize the blog post on the board.
- Students form small groups.
- Tell students to summarize the blog post by listing all the places Dan writes about. Groups should write the list on a sheet of paper.
- Begin a class discussion to check answers. Ask volunteers from each group to write their lists on the board.

(No homework today.)

>  **Teaching Tip**
> **Previewing Questions**
> It can be helpful to read the questions first before having students read a text. This will help students read for specific information and details.

Lesson 8
Student's Book pp. 90 and 91

Warm-up
Students review the theme of storytelling from Dan's blog post.
- Have students work in small groups. Ask students to review Dan's blog post on page 90.
- Ask *How do people tell stories in your culture?* Have students discuss the question in their groups.
- Elicit ideas from students, e.g., blog posts, TV shows, radio, podcasts, books, newspapers, etc.

3 🎧²⁷ Listen to the storyteller. Order the events in the story.
Students listen to a story and put the events in order.
- Preview the events in the story together as a class. Check for any comprehension problems or new vocabulary.
- Draw students' attention to the **Glossary** box on the page and read the text aloud.

Answers

top to bottom, left to right 6, 3, 2, 4, 5, 1

Audio Script
1. A long time ago, the earth was a beautiful garden, with trees and flowers. Nobody told lies.
2. But one day, one man told a lie. It was a very small lie, but it was the end of men's innocence.
3. So The spirit called all the men on earth and said, "Every time you tell a lie, I will throw one grain of sand onto earth."
4. The men said, "A grain of sand? You can't see a grain of sand!"
5. Day after day men told lies and the spirit threw grains of sand onto the earth.
6. The grains of sand formed the Sahara Desert. But here and there we can see trees and flowers, because not all men tell lies.

4 Think Fast! Name three popular stories in your culture.
Students do a one-minute timed challenge: they quickly name three popular stories in their culture.

Extension
Students discuss the sequence of events in a popular story in their culture.
- Students form pairs.
- Tell pairs to choose an important story and list the important events in the story in order.
- Students can use Activity 3 as a model.
- When the pairs are ready, bring the class together. Ask volunteers to share their lists.
- After sharing, the class can suggest additions to the list if they know the story.

Stop and Think! Critical Thinking
How important are oral stories in your country?
- Ask students *Have you ever heard someone tell a story? What oral stories have you heard?*
- Write on the board how many students have heard a story and if any, the names or descriptions of stories students have heard.
- Ask *What can we learn from oral stories told in your country?* If students struggle with the question, remind them of their ideas about what we learn from the stories of Malala and Anne Frank in Lesson 6.
- Then ask *Are these lessons important? Are oral stories an important way people teach each other in your country?* Discuss as a class.

Wrap-up
Students discuss stories from other cultures that they may know.
- Students form small groups.
- Ask students to think of stories from other cultures that they might know. Have groups list any details (characters, events, setting, etc.) that they might know on a sheet of paper. If they don't know stories from other cultures, they may use another story from their own culture.
- After a few minutes, ask groups to share their ideas with the class.

▶ **(No homework today.)**

 **Project**

> **Objective**
> Students will be able to use **past simple** to make a timeline.

Lesson 9   Student's Book p. 92

Warm-up
Students review past simple verbs on the board.
- Write the following base form verbs on the board: *go, tell, be, talk, find, see, write, make, create, meet.*
- Ask for volunteers to write the past simple forms on the board. Have one student write the answer per verb.

1 Look at the timeline. Then read the sentences and circle T (True) or F (False).
Students read the clothesline timeline and determine whether statements about it are true or false.

Answers
1. F (There is a photo and a drawing.), 2. T, 3. F (Just the major events are included in the timeline.), 4. F (The sentences are short and give the general facts.)

2 Think Fast! Where does the extra paper go?
Students do a one-minute timed challenge: they decide where another event fits on the timeline.

Answer
After the event *In 2008, I went to kindergarten.*

Wrap-up
Students think of other kinds of details John could give in his timeline.
- Tell students to think of any other kinds of details John could give in his timeline with extra paper.
- Elicit ideas from students and write them on the board, e.g., *where he was born, where he grew up, where his mom worked, when he learned to ride a bike,* etc.

Lesson 10 Student's Book p. 93

Warm-up

Students correct incorrect past simple verb forms on the board.
- Write the following incorrect past tense verbs on the board: *seed, telled, writed, meted*.
- Ask students to correct the words on the board.

Answers
saw, told, wrote, met

3 Create your own timeline and present it to your classmates.

Students create their own timelines and present them to the class.
- Read the instructions aloud as a class.
- Hand out string, paper, clothespins, and colored pencils, markers or crayons.
- Have students work independently following the steps on page 93.
- After students are done creating their timelines, split students into small groups. Ask students to take turns presenting their timelines.
- Circulate around the room and observe the presentations.

> **The Digital Touch**
>
> To incorporate digital media in the project, suggest one or more of the following:
> - Create your timeline online to print at goo.gl/PpHba5.
> - Create a timeline online to save, print or email at goo.gl/HyDTHb.
>
> Note that students should have the option to do a task on paper or digitally.

Wrap-up

Students compare their timelines in a group discussion.
- Ask the class if they noticed any interesting similarities or differences between their own timelines and their classmates' timelines. Elicit ideas from students.

➡ **Workbook p. 148, Activity 1 (Review)**

Review

Objective
Students will be able to consolidate their understanding of the vocabulary and grammar they have learned in the unit.

Lesson 11   Student's Book p. 94

✔ **Homework Check!**
Workbook page 148, Activity 1 (Review)
Answers
1 Correct the sentences using the past simple.
1. ~~were~~, It was about zombies that live in an Italian city.
2. ~~finded~~, A scientist found a medicine that made the zombies sleepy.
3. ~~where~~, ~~want~~, The special effects were really scary. I wanted to close my eyes.

Warm-up
Students review books and movies vocabulary.
- Tell students to think of words for books and movies to describe the following:
  » a funny movie
  » a book about magic and dragons
  » a movie about aliens
  » a love story

Answers
comedy, fantasy, science fiction, romance

1 Complete the words using vowels.
Students complete the words for books and movies by adding the missing vowels.
Answers
1. autobiography, 2. children's book, 3. fantasy, 4. romance, 5. action, 6. animated, 7. comedy, 8. science fiction

2 Label the book genres.
Students write the genre for each book based on its title and cover.
Answers
1. children's book, 2. fantasy, 3. autobiography, 4. romance

3 Mark (✓) the correct words to complete the sentences.
Students review genre vocabulary by marking the correct words to complete the sentences.
Answers
1. Comedy, 2. Science fiction, 3. Animated, 4. Action

4 Correct the sentences. Rewrite the underlined words.
Students replace the adjectives with the adjectives that make sense in the sentences.
Answers
1. sad, 2. boring, 3. inspirational

Wrap-up
Students review books and movies words by playing Hangman.
- Play a game of Hangman to review genre vocabulary words from page 94.
- After students guess each word, ask for some examples of books and movies in that genre: for science fiction, students could say *Star Wars* or *The Avengers*.

➡ **(No homework today.)**

96

Lesson 12 Student's Book p. 95

Warm-up

Students review past simple verbs and books and movies vocabulary by completing the sentences on the board.
- Write the following sentence on the board with a gap for students to fill:
  I _____ (see) X-Men this weekend. The X-Men have super powers. It is a _____ (genre) movie.
- Ask a student volunteer to complete the sentences on the board.

Answers

saw, science fiction

5 Complete the sentences using the past forms of the verbs below.

Students review past simple verb forms by completing the sentences.

Answers

1. studied, 2. wrote, 3. created, 4. crashed, 5. wanted

6 Complete the chart with the past forms. Then write R (Regular) or I (Irregular).

Students review regular and irregular simple past forms by completing a verb chart.

Answers

1. created, R, 2. disappeared, R, 3. explained, R, 4. found, I, 5. went, I, 6. lived, R, 7. made, I, 8. met, I, 9. saw, I, 10. started, R, 11. studied, R, 12. visited, R, 13. worked, R, 14. wrote, I

7 Complete the biography using the past forms of the verbs.

Students use past simple verb forms in narrative sequence by completing a biography.

Answers

1. was, 2. was, 3. went, was, 4. was, 5. worked, 6. made, 7. wrote

Big Question

Students are given the opportunity to revisit the Big Question and reflect on it.
- Tell students to turn to the unit opener on page 83 and look at the question, *What's your story?*
- Have students work in small groups. Ask them to discuss the question based on their work in this unit.
- Tell students to think about the biographies they have read in this unit and the timelines they made in Lesson 10. Ask students to summarize the main events in their own "stories" and how they have influenced their own lives.

Scorecard

Hand out (and/or project) a *Scorecard*. Have students fill in their *Scorecards* for this unit.

▶ **Study for the unit test.**

7 How do we contribute?

Grammar
Past simple: <u>Did</u> you <u>like</u> the work?
Yes, I <u>did</u>. No, I <u>didn't</u>. When <u>did</u> you <u>build</u> it?

Vocabulary
Professions: artist, journalist, nurse, scientist, social worker

Workplaces: community center, hospital, laboratory, office, studio

Reading
Identifying the purpose: *persuade, inform, entertain*

Speaking
Talking about a hero based on prompts

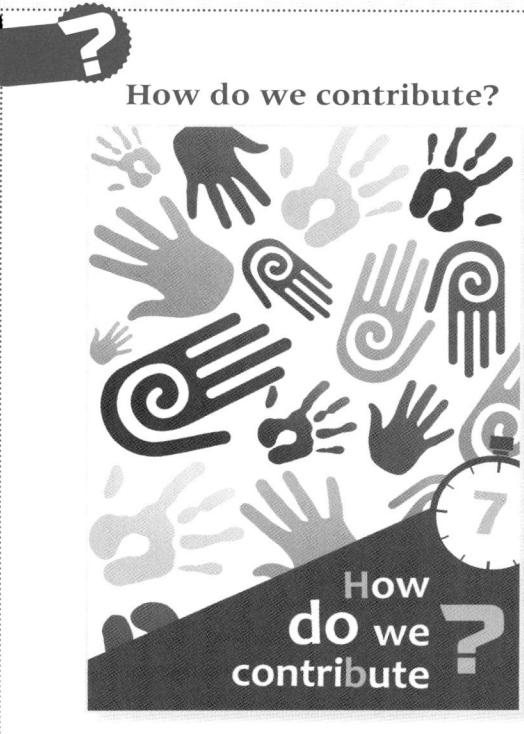

In the first lesson, read the unit title aloud and have students look carefully at the unit cover. Encourage them to think about the message in the picture. At the end of the unit, students will discuss the big question: *How do we contribute?*

Teaching Tip
Thinking About the Content
Remind students that the things they will read and learn in this unit will help them to think about the Big Question. The people they will read about contribute to their communities. Encourage students to think about how these people contribute as they progress through the unit.

 Vocabulary

Objective
Students will be able to use **professions** and **places** vocabulary to talk about careers and workplaces.

Lesson 1   Student's Book p. 98

Warm-up

Students preview pictures in the unit and think about how they relate to the Big Question.
- Have students preview the pictures in this unit. Ask *How do these people contribute?* Elicit answers from the class.

1 🎧²⁸ **Listen and number the professions.**

Students preview vocabulary for professions by listening to the audio and numbering the pictures.

Answers

left to right, top to bottom 1, 3, 4, 6, 2, 5

Audio Script

Hello, everybody! Here are six professions that change the world every day.
1. Teachers help people learn. Teachers work at schools.
2. Social workers help people with problems. They help individuals and families.
3. Scientists study the world. Some look for new medicines.
4. Nurses care for patients and administer medication. Many nurses work at hospitals.
5. Artists create and perform in different fields, like painting, music or dance.
6. Journalists investigate and present stories in magazines, newspapers, on TV and on the Internet.

2 🎧²⁸ **Number the descriptions using the professions. Then listen again to check your answers.**

Students match professions vocabulary with descriptions of what people in those professions do.

Answers

1. 5, 2. 3, 3. 6, 4. 1, 5. 5, 6. 6, 7. 2, 8. 3, 9. 4

Wrap-up

Students play a game acting out professions words.
- Ask for volunteers. Tell the volunteer to act out a professions vocabulary word. Have the class guess the word.
- The student who guesses the answer acts next. Repeat with all vocabulary words on page 98.

 **Workbook p. 150, Activities 1 and 2**

🐝 **Teaching Tip**

Using Games to Wrap Up
Ending class with a game can be a fun and engaging way to review the day's lesson. Fun games are memorable, so students may retain more of the day's lesson by reviewing with a game.

Lesson 2   Student's Book p. 99

> ✔ **Homework Check!**
> Workbook p. 150, Activities 1 and 2
>
> **Answers**
> **1 Solve the crossword puzzle. Write the professions.**
> 1. teacher, 2. nurse, 3. scientist, 4. social worker,
> 5. artist
> **2 Circle the correct professions.**
> 1. Teachers, 2. Journalists, 3. Social workers,
> 4. artists, 5. scientists

Warm-up
Students review professions vocabulary.
- In small groups, have students talk about what professions they would like to have when they grow up.
- Draw students' attention to the *Guess What!* box on page 98. Tell them to read the information.

3 Write the professions.
Students complete the descriptions with professions vocabulary.

Answers

1. artist, 2. nurse, 3. scientist, 4. journalist,
5. teacher, 6. social worker

4 🎧²⁹ Listen and write the professions.
Students listen to the audio and write the profession for each person.

Answers

1. nurse, 2. scientist, 3. teacher

Audio Script
1. I'm reading this book about famous professional women from the past. It's really cool!
   The book starts with Florence Nightingale. She was a British nurse. She helped soldiers during a war between Russia and the British Empire.
2. The next woman is Marie Curie. She was a French scientist. She discovered the properties of radioactivity. Madame Curie was the first woman to win the Nobel Prize!
3. Finally, Anne Sullivan was an American teacher. She became famous for teaching Helen Keller. Helen didn't see and didn't hear, and didn't speak. But Anne Sullivan taught Helen how to communicate and read braille.

5 Think Fast! What do the people in Activity 4 have in common?
Students do a two-minute timed challenge: they discuss and make a list of the things Marie Curie, Florence Nightingale, and Anne Sullivan had in common.

Answers

Answers will vary.

Wrap-up
Students review professions vocabulary by playing a game.
- Students form pairs.
- Tell Student A to choose a profession without telling his or her partner which one it is.
- Tell Student B to ask Student A questions to find out what his or her secret profession is.
- Students switch roles and play again.
- Have pairs compete to see who can guess their partner's profession using the fewest questions.

⟹ **Workbook p. 150, Activity 3**

 Grammar

Objective
Students will be able to use **past simple** in affirmative statements, negative statements and questions.

Lesson 3   Student's Book p. 100

✔ **Homework Check!**
Workbook p. 150, Activity 3

Answers
3 Complete the sentences using the words below.
1. hospitals, 2. laboratories, 3. community centers, 4. studios, 5. offices

Warm-up
Students review the places where people work by writing the professions words from page 98 on the board. Ask students where each person works. Write their answers on the board.

1 Complete the interview with the verbs in past.
Students practice using some common verbs in past by completing sentences in an interview.
- Before students begin, ask students to give the base form of each verb (*join, learn, make, talk*).
- Draw students' attention to the words in red. Explain that we ask questions in the past simple by using *did* and a base form verb. To answer in the positive, use *did*. To answer in the negative, we use *didn't*.

Answers
1. joined, 2. talked, 3. learned, 4. made

2 Write two more questions for Zach. Use the past simple.
Students use the past simple (*did* or *didn't*) to complete the questions and answers.

Answers
1. did, 2. Did, did, didn't

3 Think Fast! In your notebook, write two more questions for Zach using the past simple.
Students do a two-minute timed challenge: they write two more questions for Zach in their notebooks, using the past simple. After two minutes, elicit questions from students. Then ask students how they think Zach would respond.

Answers
Answers will vary.

Extension
Students ask and answer questions with a partner about a funny experience they had.
- Have the partner ask three questions using the past simple (yes/no questions) to get more information.
- Once the student answers using the past simple, students switch roles.

Wrap-up
Students ask and answer questions for Zach in small groups.
- Students form small groups.
- Tell students to share the two extra questions for Zach they wrote in Activity 3 with their groups.
- Have the groups discuss how they think Zach would answer each question and write answers to all of the group members' questions in their notebooks.

 Workbook p. 151, Activity 1

Lesson 4   Student's Book p. 101

> ✔ **Homework Check!**
> Workbook p. 151, Activity 1
>
> **Answers**
> **1 Complete the questions in past tense using the verbs in parentheses.**
> 1. did you become, 2. did you do, 3. Did you receive, 4. did you learn

Warm-up

Students review questions and answers in past simple.
- Write the following questions and answers on the board:
  » *Did you walk to school today?*
  » *Yes, I did. / No, I didn't.*
- Ask students to choose their answer. Then ask students to raise their hands if they answered *Yes, I did*. Count the students. Then ask students to raise their hands if they answered *No, I didn't*.
- Ask volunteers to share how they got to school today in the past simple.

4 Unscramble the questions. Then answer and write your score.

Students unscramble the questions independently and write them on the lines; then they answer each and write the number of green bars corresponding to each answer in the *Me* column.

Answers
1. How did you get to school yesterday?, 2. Where did you throw your garbage yesterday?, 3. Did you do any volunteer work last year?, 4. Did you turn off your computer yesterday?, 5. Did you say "thank you" to someone this morning?

5 Work with a partner. Ask and answer the questions in the quiz.

Students do a speaking activity: they ask a partner the questions and write the number of green bars corresponding to their partner's answers in the *My partner* column.

Answers
Answers will vary.

6 Add up your scores and check your result.

Students add up their scores for all of the survey questions and read the result corresponding to their score.

Extension
Read each score description aloud and ask how many students got each result. Tally the numbers on the board. Then ask students if they agree or disagree with their score descriptions. Why or why not?

Wrap-up

Students review past simple statements (positive and negative) and questions by creating a news story together.
- Students form small groups.
- One student volunteers to think of an event for a news story related to work or people contributing to the community.
- If students have trouble thinking of an event, some suggestions to make are *a nurse delivered a baby on a bus*, *a social worker organized an after-school program for teens at the community center* or *a scientist discovered a cure for cancer*.
- Students go around the group, taking turns asking and answering questions to develop their news story: Student A: *A nurse delivered a baby on a bus*. Student B: *Did the nurse work at the local hospital?* Student C: *No, he didn't. He worked in another city.* Student D: *Was the baby a boy or a girl?* Student E: *The baby was a girl.*
- Invite groups to share their news story with the class.

➡ **Workbook p. 151, Activity 2**

Objective
Students will be able to identify the purpose of a text from three options: to persuade, to inform or to entertain. They will also be able to talk about a hero using prompts.

Lesson 5 — Student's Book p. 102

> ✔ **Homework Check!**
> Workbook p. 151, Activity 2
> **Answers**
> **2 Reread the text on page 100. Mark the statements *T* (True) or *F* (False). Then rewrite the incorrect sentences.**
> 1. F, Zach joined GoGreen when he was 11.,
> 2. F, He met a volunteer at his school., 3. T, 4. F, He took some classes about trees., 5. F, He made good friends.

Warm-up
Students prepare for the lesson by discussing questions about heroes.
- Ask *What is a hero? Who can be a hero in real life?*
- Elicit ideas from students.

1 Read the article quickly. Mark (✓) the purpose of the text.
Students read an article quickly to identify its purpose.
- Draw students' attention to the **Be Strategic!** box on page 102 and read the information aloud.
- Before students read the article, read answers 1, 2 and 3 aloud.
- Elicit ideas from students and ask why they chose their answers.

Answer
2

2 How did these people contribute to *ReMind*? Match the parts of the sentences.
Students read the article again more carefully and do a matching activity to identify the actions of people mentioned in the text.

Answers
Natalie's mother built the prototype for the app with Natalie., *Natalie's grandfather* inspired Natalie to create *ReMind*., *Ms. Williams* helped Natalie create the concept for the app.

Wrap-up
Students describe any heroes they know of in books, movies or TV. For each hero named, ask the class *What makes this person a hero?*

▶ **Workbook p. 152, Activities 3 and 4**

Lesson 6   Student's Book p. 103

> ✔ **Homework Check!**
>
> Workbook p. 152, Activities 3 and 4
>
> **Answers**
> **3 Read about Anne Sullivan. Then read the sentences below and correct them in your notebook.**
> 1. She didn't teach Helen Keller to play the piano. She taught Helen Keller to communicate.
> 2. She didn't help Keller study at primary school. She helped Keller study at university.
> 3. She didn't travel with Keller around the world. She traveled around the United States.
> 4. Anne Sullivan didn't die in 1836. She died in 1936.
> **4 Read Anne Sullivan's biography again. Then complete the questions.**
> 1. she move, 2. did she have, 3. did she study, 4. did they meet

Warm-up
Have students review the previous lesson's article and questions in the past simple.
- Write the following questions on the board:
  » Did Natalie's teacher help her build the prototype?
  » Did Natalie's mother help Natalie create the concept for the app?
- Elicit answers from students.

Answers
No, she didn't. Her mother did.
No, she didn't. Ms. Williams did.

3 Read and answer with a partner: Who is Matt's hero? Why?
Students read the text independently and then discuss the question with a partner. Go over students' ideas as a class.

Answers
Matt's hero is his sister Madison, because she is a brave and strong cancer survivor.

4 Who is your personal hero? Complete the chart.
Students personalize the theme by completing the information in the chart about a personal hero.

Answers
Answers will vary.

5 Work in small groups. Ask your partners about their heroes. Use your notes from Activity 4 to talk about yours.
Students form small groups and ask and answers questions about groups members' heroes using their notes from Activity 4.

Stop and Think! Critical Thinking
What can you learn from personal heroes?
- Students stay in the groups they formed for Activity 5 and make lists of things they can learn from each group member's personal hero.
- Ask one student from each group to share their list with the class.

Wrap-up
Ask students to think about the heroes their classmates described in Activity 5. Ask *What things do these heroes have in common?* Elicit ideas from students.

▶ **Workbook p. 153, Activities 1–3**

Preparing for the Next Lesson
Ask students to watch an introduction to volunteering in Tanzania: goo.gl/S5ZS7R or invite them to look around on the *TIME for Kids* website: goo.gl/JiSP3f.

Culture

Objective
Students will be able to explore what a linguistic community is through a reading about volunteering abroad.

Wrap-up
Students respond to the text with a personalization activity.
- Ask students what they thought the most interesting part of the text was. Ask them what they would like to see in Tanzania.

➡ **(No homework today.)**

Lesson 7   Student's Book pp. 104 and 105

✔ Homework Check!
Workbook p. 153, Activities 1–3

Answers
1 Read the text. Then mark (✓) the best answer.
a
2 Number the text about a personal hero.
top to bottom 3, 2, 1, 4
3 In your notebook, write about a partner's personal hero.
Answers will vary.

Warm-up
To preview the content of this lesson, have students look at the pictures on pages 104 and 105.
- Ask students to describe the things they see. (Answer: a desert, friends, traditional clothing, a map of Africa, etc.)
- Ask *Where is Tanzania? What is Swahili?*

106

1 Read about a girl's experience in Tanzania. Mark (✓) the best title for the text.
Students read the text and choose the best title. Elicit answers from students and ask them why they chose their answers.

Answer
3

2 Complete the information with words from the text.
Students scan the text for specific information and use it to complete the luggage tag.

Answers
1. Chloe, 2. Tanzania, 3. Serengeti National Park

Extension
Students write about a trip.
- Have students write about a trip they took. This could be in another country, or even near home.
- Students may use the text on page 104 as a model.
- Tell students to describe the places they saw, the people they met, and the things they learned.
- Encourage volunteers to share their stories with the class.
- Note: Students may make up their stories if they can't think of a place they have visited.

Lesson 8
Student's Book pp. 104 and 105

Warm-up
Students scan the text for place names.
- Ask students to review the text on page 104.
- Have students underline the different places mentioned in the text.
- Elicit answers from students.

3 🎧³⁰ Listen and write the English words on the map.
Students match Swahili and English words in a listening activity.
- Play the audio and have students write the English words for places in nature on the map.

Answers

ziwa lake, *simba* lion, *tembo* elephant, *mlima* mountain, *ufukoni* beach, *jiji* city

Audio Script
JAMBO! I'm Chloe.
People in Tanzania speak 125 different languages.
People speak a local language. Swahili is for communication with people who don't speak the local language.
I learned some words in Swahili. Listen:
ZIWA is lake.
SIMBA is lion.
TEMBO is elephant.
MLIMA is mountain.
UFUKONI is beach.
And JIJI is city.

4 Read and answer the questions with a partner.
Students work with a partner to discuss the topic of the reading in relation to their own countries.
- Elicit answers from the class and discuss their answers and reasoning.

Answers
Answers will vary.

Stop and Think! Critical Thinking
How do languages connect people?
- Tell students to think about how their culture and native language connect them to each other.
- Additionally, ask students *How does learning English bring you together as a community?*

Wrap-up
Students do a timed memory challenge.
- Have students close their books and notebooks.
- Ask *How many Swahili words can you remember? What are the English translations?*
- Give students 2 minutes to respond. (Use your Stopwatch app to time it.)
- The first student to raise his or her hand and give the most Swahili words and translations from the article wins.
- Now ask *Is it easier for you to remember new English words or new Swahili words? Why?*

⏩ **(No homework today.)**

 **Project**

Objective
Students will be able to develop a plan to solve a problem in the community.

Lesson 9   Student's Book p. 106

Warm-up

To prepare students for the Project on pages 106 and 107, ask the class *What are some ways we can help our community?* Elicit answers.

1 Write the steps in order. Refer to page 102 if necessary.
Students order events from an article in time sequence.

Answers

7, *1*, 6, 2, 4, 3, 5

2 Read and mark (✓) the sentences that are true for your community. Then add two more sentences.
Students read statements and think about whether they are true for their community. They write two more sentences that are true for their community. Invite students to share examples and reasons for their answers.

Answers

Answers will vary.

Wrap-up

Students practice identifying problems and proposing solutions.
- Ask students *What are some problems our school has?*
- Elicit answers from the class. Examples: *The classrooms are too small. The school lunch is bad.*
- Write a few of the problems on the board.
- Students form small groups.
- Assign each group a school problem to solve.
- Tell groups to make a list of the causes of the problem and identify solutions that address each cause.
- Invite groups to present their problem and solution to the class.

Lesson 10 Student's Book p. 107

Warm-up
Students review problems in their community.
- Ask students to look back at their answers to Activity 2 on page 106. Review the problems students think their community has with the class.
- For each problem, ask *What are some causes of this problem?*
- Then ask, *How do communities solve problems?* Elicit ideas from the class.

3 Form small groups. Answer the questions.
Students form small groups and discuss the questions. Tell students to reach an agreement on their answers for each question and to have a volunteer write the group's answers down in a notebook.

Answers

Answers will vary.

4 Present your plan to the class.
Students present their ideas from Activity 3 to the class.
- As groups present, tell the other students to take notes.
- Then tell the class to pose questions to the presenting group. Do the same for each group.

5 Present the results of your actions in one month.
Tell groups to think about what the results of their actions would be in one month.
- Allow groups to discuss for five minutes and take notes. Then ask a volunteer from each group to share their results.
- Ask *What other solutions could also work?*

> **The Digital Touch**
> To incorporate digital media in the project, suggest one or more of the following:
> - Students can create their presentations in PowerPoint or Google Slides.
> - Students can record their presentations using a smart phone or a tablet.
>
> Note that students should have the option to do a task on paper or digitally.

Wrap-up
Ask students to vote on the most important problem their classmates described today. Elicit reasons for students' choices.

 **Workbook p. 152, Activity 1 (Review)**

> **Teaching Tip**
> **Encouraging Peer Editing**
> Peer editing is a good way to help students take ownership of their learning. Encourage students to correct each other's work and to offer each other constructive criticism. Advise students to help each other improve their work without hurting each other's feelings.

Review

Objective
Students will be able to consolidate their understanding of the vocabulary and grammar they have learned in the unit.

Wrap-up
Students review words for professions by playing a game. Ask volunteers to act out different words from Activity 1 and have the class guess the profession.

➠ **(No homework today.)**

Lesson 11   Student's Book p. 108

> ✔ **Homework Check!**
> Workbook p. 152, Activity 1 (Review)
> **Answers**
> **1 In your notebook, answer the questions.**
> Answers will vary.

Warm-up

Students review professions vocabulary words.
- Say *I work in a hospital.* Ask *Who am I?* Students should think of who works in that location and give the profession. (Answer: nurse)
- Continue with the other professions words: *laboratory / scientist, community center / social worker, studio / artist, office / journalist, school / teacher.*

1 Complete the puzzle with six professions. Then complete the sentence using the word in the green box.

Students review professions vocabulary by completing a crossword puzzle.

Answers
1. social worker, 2. teacher, 3. journalist, 4. nurse, 5. scientist, 6. artist; governess

2 Label the workplaces.

Students review places vocabulary by labeling photos with the workplaces shown in them.

Answers
1. office, 2. hospital, 3. school, 4. community center, 5. laboratory, 6. art studio

3 Read the sentences and correct the workplaces.

Students correct sentences with the appropriate place where people of each profession work.

Answers
1. Nurses work in hospitals., 2. Scientist work at laboratories., 3. Social workers work at community centers., 4. Artist work in art studios., 5. Journalists work in offices., 6. Teachers work in schools.

Lesson 12   Student's Book p. 109

Warm-up

Students review questions and answers using past simple.

- Write the following sentences on the board with gaps for students to fill:
  Q: _____
  A: Yes, Tina went to school.
  Q: Did James pass the test?
  A: No, _____

- Have students complete the question and answer in their notebooks. The first student to correctly complete the question and answer wins.

Answers

Did Tina go to school?
James didn't pass the test. / he didn't.

4 Match the questions to the answers.

Students review past simple questions by matching questions with their corresponding answers.

Answers

1. b, 2. e, 3. d, 4. a, 5. c

5 Unscramble the questions.

Students form questions from cues using past simple.

Answers

1. Did Marie Curie live in France all her life?, 2. Why did she move to France?, 3. When did she start at Sorbonne?, 4. Did Marie Curie have any children?, 5. Where did she die?

6 Change the sentences into negative sentences (−) or questions (?).

Students rewrite affirmative past simple sentences as negative sentences or questions in past simple.

Answers

1. My mother didn't study at Harvard University., 2. Did Alice live in Spain for three years?, 3. Tyler didn't go on vacation last month., 4. Did Sam's dad work last Saturday?

 Big Question

Students are given the opportunity to revisit the Big Question and reflect on it.

- Ask students to turn to the unit opener on page 97 and look at the question *How do we contribute?*
- Have students work in small groups. Ask them to discuss the question based on their work in this unit.
- Tell students to think about the things they read and discussed in this unit. How did the people in the unit contribute to their communities? How do people in different professions contribute to communities?

⭐ Scorecard

Hand out (and/or project) a *Scorecard*. Have students fill in their *Scorecards* for this unit.

▶ **Study for the unit test.**

 8 How do we spend our free time?

Grammar

Have to: My sister <u>has to</u> walk the dog. I <u>have to</u> clean my room.

Future: *going to*: My parents are <u>going to travel</u> this weekend.

Vocabulary

Chores and Free-time Activities: clean (your) room, do the dishes, do homework, go to the park, hang out with friends, play video games, take out the trash, walk the dog, watch a movie

Emotions: angry, bored, excited, happy, nervous, sad, scared, tired

Reading

Reading for specific information

Speaking

Inviting, accepting and rejecting an invitation

How do we spend our free time?

In the first lesson, read the unit title aloud and have students look carefully at the unit cover. Encourage them to think about the message in the picture. At the end of the unit, students will discuss the big question: *How do we spend our free time?*

Teaching Tip
Recycling Language
When doing less structured activities like class discussions, try to include and use vocabulary, grammar and topics learned in past units. Recycling language can help strengthen students' understanding. As the old saying goes, "Use it or lose it!"

113

 **Vocabulary**

Objective
Students will be able to use **actions** and **adjectives** vocabulary to talk about how we spend our time.

Lesson 1   Student's Book pp. 112 and 113

Warm-up
Students preview the theme of the unit.
- Have students look at the unit cover again on page 111.
- Ask students *What is free time? When do you have free time?*
- Ask students if they recognize the things the people are doing in the pictures. Ask *Do you do these things for fun, or are they work?*

1 Look and complete the activities.
Students practice collocations for actions vocabulary by completing labels for photos.

Answers
1. walk the dog, 2. do the dishes, 3. clean your room, 4. take out the trash, 5. watch a movie, 6. hang out with friends, 7. play video games, 8. go to the park

2 Mark (✓) when you do these activities.
In a personalization activity, students mark which days they do each activity.

 114

Answers
Answers will vary.

Stop and Think! Critical Thinking
Share your information with a classmate. Who does the most chores?
- Draw students' attention to the **Stop and Think!** box on page 113 and read the question aloud.
- Have students work with a partner to ask the questions (for example, *When do you clean your room?*) Students should say when or how often they clean their rooms (for example, *I clean my room on Monday, Wednesday and Saturday.*).
- When pairs have finished comparing their activities, ask each pair in a whole-class discussion *Who does the most chores?* Elicit answers from the class.
- Ask if there are chores on the list that no one does or that almost everyone does. Read each activity on the list and have students raise their hands if they do that chore. Tally the results on the board and see which chore is done by most students.

Wrap-up
Students classify actions.
- Ask students to look at the chart in Activity 2 again. Ask *Are these activities fun or work?*
- Have students write *C* for chores and *F* for fun activities next to each activity. Then elicit answers from the class.

▸ **Workbook p. 154, Activities 1 and 2**

Lesson 2 — Student's Book pp. 112 and 113

> ✔ **Homework Check!**
> Workbook p. 154, Activities 1 and 2
> **Answers**
> **1 Circle the correct words.**
> 1. walk, 2. watch, 3. go, 4. clean, 5. hang out,
> 6. take out, 7. play
> **2 Classify the activities from Activity 1.**
> *Chores* walk the dog, clean your room, take out the trash
> *Free-time Activities* watch movies, go to the park, hang out with friends, play video games

Warm-up
Students review chores and free-time activities by identifying actions. Act out the activities from page 112. After students guess the activity, ask *Is it a chore? Or is it a free-time activity?*

3 🎧³¹ **Listen and circle the correct emoticon. Then complete the sentences.**
Students are introduced to adjectives vocabulary for emotions by circling the correct emoticon for the emotion mentioned in the audio and completing the sentences with the correct words.

Answers
1. happy, 2. scared, 3. tired, 4. nervous, 5. bored

Audio Script
1. Mel
   GIRL 1: Yes! I finished the game! Woo-hoo!
   GIRL 2: That's great, Mel! This game is so difficult.
2. Jessica
   GIRL: I-I-I don't like this movie. Let's watch something else…
   BOY: Come on, Jess…
3. Thomas and Finn
   BOY 1: Phew… There are so many leaves… and this yard is so big…
   BOY 2: Yeah… Let's stop and rest.
4. Lucas
   MAN: OK. We're going to start the test now. Just leave a pen on your desks.
   BOY: I need to do well on this test, I really need a good grade.
   MAN: Lucas, is everything ok?
   BOY: Y-Yes, Mr. Brown.
5. Josh
   BOY: There's nothing good on TV… I think I'm going to sleep…

4 **Read and write an adjective. How do you feel?**
Students practice using adjectives for emotions by reading the sentences and writing an adjective from the list on the right of page 113.

Answers
1. scared, 2. sad, 3. tired, 4. happy

> **Extension**
> Students express their feelings about chores and free-time activities. Tell students to write two sentences using vocabulary for actions and adjectives for emotions. Ask *How do you feel when you do these activities?* Encourage volunteers to share their sentences with the class.

Wrap-up
Students review adjectives vocabulary for emotions by playing a game.
- Have students close their books. Make a face to match one of the words for emotions on page 113.
- As students guess answers, ask them to give a sentence using the word: *When I…, I feel…* The first student to guess each word correctly gets a point.
- Alternatively, have students take turns making faces to match each emotion. The student who guesses the emotion correctly is next to act out an emotion of his or her choosing.

▶ **Workbook pp. 154 and 155, Activities 3 and 4**

Grammar

Objectives
Students will be able to use **have to** to express obligations and **going to** to talk about future plans.

Lesson 3 Student's Book p. 114

✔ Homework Check!
Workbook pp. 154 and 155, Activities 3 and 4
Answers
3 Solve the crossword.
0. tired, 1. bored, 2. scared, 3. angry, 4. excited,
5. sad, 6. happy, 7. nervous
4 How do you feel? Complete the sentences.
(Answers will vary.) Examples: 1. happy, 2. sad,
3. happy / excited, 4. Answers will vary.

Warm-up
Students preview the lesson.
- Ask students *What do you see in the illustration on page 114?* (Answer: A refrigerator with magnets and a note on it.)
- Ask *What is the purpose of this note? Who is it to, and who is it from? Do you ever get notes like this?*

1 **Listen and write *Aiden* and/or *John*.**
Students are introduced to *have to* for obligation. They listen to the audio and write *Aiden* and/or *John* next to each task to identify who is assigned to perform each task.
Answers
top to bottom Aiden and John, John, Aiden, Aiden

Audio Script
FATHER: OK, Aiden. This is the list of chores you and your brother have to do this week. You and John have to clean your room. You both have to do it, because you share the room.
AIDEN: OK, Dad.
FATHER: And you have to walk Rufus…
AIDEN: No, not me! I always walk Rufus. It's John's turn.
FATHER: All right, so John has to walk Rufus. Then you have to do the dishes after dinner, Aiden.
AIDEN: OK, OK…
FATHER: And you have to go to the supermarket with me, Aiden. Your brother always helps me with that, but you never go with us.
AIDEN: OK, Dad, OK.

2 Circle the correct form.
Students identify the correct form of *have to* to complete the sentences. Draw students' attention to the **Have to – Obligation** box on page 114 and read the information aloud.
Answers
1. have to, 2. has to, 3. has to, 4. have to, 5. have to

3 Write four sentences about the chores you and people in your family have to do.
Students practice using *have to* in a personalization activity by writing four sentences about the chores they and the people in their families have to do. Students should use the words in the box.
Answers
Answers will vary.

Wrap-up
Students review the use of *have to* by correcting sentences. Write the following sentences on the board:
I has to do homework tonight.
We has to eat lunch every day.
You has to do the dishes.
They have to go to school.
Tell students to decide if the sentences are correct or incorrect and correct the incorrect sentences in their notebooks. The first student to correct the incorrect sentences wins.
Answers
I <u>have</u> to do homework tonight., We <u>have</u> to eat lunch every day., You <u>have</u> to do the dishes., correct

▶ Workbook p. 155, Activities 1 and 2

Teaching Tip
Encouraging Peer Correction
Asking students to share their writing with their classmates can make them a little nervous. Let them know that correcting their work is not a judgment on them as people. It is a way to learn and do better in English. People often learn better when they make mistakes.

Lesson 4   Student's Book p. 115

✔ **Homework Check!**
Workbook p. 155, Activities 1 and 2
Answers
1 Mark the sentences correct (✓) or incorrect (✗). Rewrite the incorrect ones.
1. (✓), 2. (✓), 3. (✗) has We have to do our homework before playing video games., 4. (✓),
5. (✗) has Students in Japan have to clean their classrooms.
2 Read the chat and write sentences. Use *have to* or *has to*.
1. Hunter has to make the cake., 2. Katie has to make fruit juice., 3. Julia and Alex have to decorate Kim's garage for the party., 4. Kim has to prepare the playlist., 5. Gabriel and Luke have to distract Sean.

Warm-up

Students review *have to* by giving solutions to problems. For example, say *The trash can is full.* and ask students to give advice using *have to: You have to take out the trash.* Other examples: *The dishes are dirty.* (You have to do the dishes.) *The dog needs to go outside.* (You have to walk the dog).

4 🎧³³ **Listen and correct the schedule for next week.**
Students are introduced to *going to* by reading a schedule and correcting it based on the audio.
Answers

Monday evening ~~Do homework~~ Do the dishes,
Tuesday evening ~~Do the dishes~~ Do homework,
Wednesday evening ~~Do homework~~ Do the dishes,
Thursday evening ~~Do the dishes~~ Do homework,
Friday afternoon ~~Free!~~ Go to the supermarket,
Friday evening ~~Free!~~ Do the dishes,
Saturday morning Clean our room,
Saturday afternoon ~~Go to the supermarket~~ Go the park with friends

Audio Script
FATHER: Right, Aiden. Let's review when you are going to do the chores. When are you going to clean your room?
AIDEN: I'm going to do it on Saturday morning. Is John going to help me?
FATHER: Yes, he is. He's going to clean, too. When are you going to do the dishes?
AIDEN: I'm going to do the dishes on Monday, Wednesday and Friday evenings.
FATHER: And what are you going to do on Tuesday and Thursday?
AIDEN: I'm going to do my homework, Dad.
FATHER: All right. And we're going to go to the supermarket on Saturday afternoon.
AIDEN: But I'm going to the park with my friends on Saturday afternoon.
FATHER: I forgot. So we're not going to the supermarket on Saturday, then. Let's go on Friday.
AIDEN: Thanks, Dad.

5 Complete the sentences with the correct verbs.
Students practice *going to* by completing the sentences with the verbs *do, go* or *play*.
Answers
1. play, 2. do, 3. go, 4. go

6 Look and answer the questions about Aiden's schedule.
Students write sentences with *going to* by reading and answering the questions.
Answers
1. Aiden is going to play soccer on Monday and Wednesday afternoons., 2. Aiden is going to go to guitar lessons., 3. No, Aiden is not going to do the dishes on Tuesday and Thursday evening., 4. Yes, Aiden is going to the supermarket on Friday afternoon., 5. Aiden and John are going to clean their room on Saturday morning.

Wrap-up

Students review *going to* by writing sentences with three activities they are going to do this week and one activity they are not going to do this week. Students can use Activity 5 as a model. Elicit answers from the class.

▶ **Workbook p. 156, Activities 3–5**

Reading & Speaking

Objectives
Students will be able to predict information that they will find in a text. They will also be able to invite others to an event and accept and reject invitations.

Lesson 5
Student's Book p. 116

> ✔ **Homework Check!**
> Workbook p. 156, Activities 3–5
>
> **Answers**
> **3 Complete the sentences using *be going to*.**
> 1. is going to organize, 2. are going to travel, am going to stay, 3. am not going to watch, 4. is not going to play
>
> **4 Write sentences about Anna's plans.**
> 1. Anna is going to study for the history test., 2. Anna is going to go to the supermarket with Mom / her mom., 3. Anna is going to help Mom and Dad / her mom and dad prepare dinner.
>
> **5 Write questions. Ask about the words in bold.**
> 1. Who are you going to travel with?, 2. Where are you going to stay?, 3. Are you going to travel by bus?

Warm-up
To preview this lesson, ask students to look at the pictures on pages 116 and 117. Ask *What are some things people have to do to prepare for a party?*

1 Mark (✓) the kind of information you expect in party invitations.
Students preview the reading by marking the kind of information they expect in party invitations.

Answers
1, 2, 4, 5

2 Read the invitation and check your answers.
Have students read the invitation independently and check their answers. Ask *Were you right? What was different?*

3 Imagine you received the invitation. Answer the questions.
Draw students' attention to the **Be Strategic!** box on page 116 and read the information aloud. Do the first questions together as a model. Ask *What kind of word will tell us what kind of party it is?* Elicit answers from the class.

Answers
1. It is a surprise party. / It is a birthday party. / It is a pool party., 2. No, it is Madison's birthday party., 3. You need to take a swimsuit, flip-flops and towel., 4. The party is going to take place at 2 p.m. on Saturday, July 1., 5. No, the party is going to happen at Madison's house., 6. No, you cannot talk to Madison about it because the party is a surprise.

Extension
Students make their own party invitations.
- Tell students to choose an event (for example, a birthday, graduation, a pet's birthday, etc.) and write their own party invitations for it.
- Ask students to use the invitation to Madison's Pool Party as a model and include the information people would expect to see in an invitation. After students finish, ask volunteers to share with the class.

Wrap-up
Students review what kind of information they expect to find in an invitation.
- Write the following invitation on the board, which is missing important information.
  Come to Andrew's birthday party! The party is at Mike's house on Saturday.
- Tell students to work in pairs and to figure out what information is missing. Elicit answers from the class.

Answers
date, time, location, details about the type of party and what you should bring

➡ **Workbook p. 157, Activity 1**

> 💭 **Teaching Tip**
> **Managing Fast Finishers**
> Some students complete activities more quickly than others, so it's a good idea to have a few extra activities on hand, otherwise these students may become bored and disruptive. One set of activities designed for fast finishers are the *Just for Fun* pages. Students can work on these individually and then check their answers in the back of the Student's Book. The *Just for Fun* activities for this unit are on page 124.

Lesson 6 Student's Book p. 117

> ✔ **Homework Check!**
> Workbook p. 157, Activity 1
> **Answers**
> **1 Read the conversation. Then write *T* (True) or *F* (False) and correct the false sentences.**
> 1. F (The party is going to be on Friday, June 24.), 2. F (It's going to be a costume party.), 3. T, 4. F (Natsuki is going to dress up like Temari.)

Warm-up
Students preview the lesson by discussing the information they expect in an oral invitation. Say *Imagine you don't receive a written invitation to an event, but your friend calls and invites you. What information do you need to decide if you can go?* Elicit answers from the class. (Possible answers: Type of event, date and time, location, what you should bring.)

4 🎧³⁴ **Listen and read along.**
Students learn how to accept and reject invitations by listening to and reading dialogues.

Audio Script
Inviting someone
GIRL: Would you like to go to Madison's birthday party?
BOY: When is it?
GIRL: It's on Saturday, July 1st.
Accepting an invitation
BOY: Sure, I'd love to. What time?
GIRL: At 2 p.m.
BOY: And where is it?
GIRL: At Madison's house. It's a pool party.
BOY: Great!
GIRL: But don't tell Madison, OK? It's a surprise party.
BOY: Of course!
Rejecting an invitation
BOY: Sorry, I can't. I'm going to travel with my parents on Friday.
GIRL: That's too bad… Maybe next time.
BOY: Sure.
GIRL: But don't tell Madison, OK? It's a surprise party.
BOY: OK!

5 **In pairs, practice the conversations.**
Students work with a partner and practice the conversations. Students switch roles and practice again.

6 **Work in small groups. Take turns inviting to a party and accepting or rejecting invitations.**
Separate students into small groups. Ask students to take turns in their groups inviting to a party and accepting or rejecting invitations. Students should not just read the conversations in Activity 5, but use the instructions for speakers A and B in the activity to guide their conversations.

Wrap-up
Ask students to reflect on their conversations Ask *What is the best way to reject an invitation?* Elicit answers from the class.

 Workbook p. 157, Activity 2

Preparing for the Next Lesson
Ask students to watch an introduction to Hawaiian luaus: goo.gl/kJYgJM.

 **Culture**

Objectives
Students will be able to talk about the features of a traditional Hawaiian celebration and discuss the value of celebrations for communities.

Lesson 7   Student's Book pp. 118 and 119

> ✔ **Homework Check!**
> Workbook p. 157, Activity 2
> **Answers**
> **2 Create an invitation for Yuna's party.**
> Answers will vary.

Warm-up

To preview this lesson, ask students *What is a luau? Have you ever heard of one before? What do you think people do at a luau?* Elicit answers from the class.

1 Think Fast! Look at the pictures. In your notebook, write 10 words of things you see.

Students do a three-minute timed challenge: they look at the pictures and write 10 words of the things they see.

Answers

Answers will vary.

2 Read the article. Then match.

 Students read an article and do a matching activity to check comprehension.

Answers

top to bottom 2, 5, 3, 1, 4

Wrap-up

Students personalize the topic in a class discussion. Ask *What parts of a luau are similar to celebrations in your country? What is different?* Elicit answers from the class.

➭ **(No homework today.)**

Lesson 8   Student's Book pp. 118 and 119

Warm-up

Students play a game to see what they remember about the text from the previous lesson. Separate students into small teams and pretend you are in a game show. Tell students to close their books. Ask questions like *What is something you eat at a luau? Where do you have a luau? When did luaus start? Did a king or a president start the luau tradition?* The first team to raise their hands and give a correct answer to each question gets a point. The team with the most points wins.

3 Label the five pictures above using the highlighted words.

Students review words from the article by labeling the five pictures with the highlighted words in the article.

Answers

left to right poi, outdoors, ukelele, taro plants, hula

4 Organize a luau. Copy the table in your notebook and write who does what.

Student groups organize a luau by drawing the table in their notebooks and deciding who in their group does what tasks to organize it.

- After 5–10 minutes, ask groups to share their plans for the luau.
- Draw students' attention to the **Guess What!** box and read the information aloud. Ask students *How many people do you think were invited to the King's luau to eat so much food?*

Stop and Think! Critical Thinking

Are Hawaiians always on vacation? Why do you think so?

- Draw students' attention to the **Stop and Think!** box on page 119 and read the question aloud.
- Say *Hawaiians live on beautiful islands full of beaches. Are they on vacation?*
- Guide students to understand that Hawaiians live daily lives like everyone else. They go to school and work.
- Ask *Where do you think Hawaiians go for vacation?*

Wrap-up

Ask students what else they would do to plan for their luau. Ask *Is there anything else you have to do?* Elicit answers from the class.

➡ **(No homework today.)**

 **Project**

Objective
Students will be able to carry out and present a survey.

Lesson 9   Student's Book p. 120

Warm-up
Ask students to look back at page 118. Ask *What kind of text is this?* Elicit answers from the class. (Answer: an article)

1 Look at the text below and mark (✓) the text type.
Students preview text types (surveys and articles) and mark the correct text type.

Answer
a survey

2 Circle T (True) or F (False).
Read the statements aloud and have students determine whether each is true or false.

Answers
1. T, 2. F (Respondents answer the questions in a survey.), 3. F (You use check marks to indicate the answers.)

> **Extension**
> Students practice analyzing the results of the survey on page 120 by making bar charts.
> • Have students draw bar charts like the one on page 121 showing how many students marked each category.
> • Ask *How do bar charts help us communicate and understand information?*

Wrap-up
Ask students *What do people use surveys for? Where else have you seen a survey?* Elicit answers from the class.

Lesson 10   Student's Book p. 121

Warm-up
Ask students *What topics do you want to find out about? Would a survey help you?* Elicit answers from students and note their ideas on the board.

3 Work in small groups. Create and carry out a survey.
Students create a survey, carry it out and organize their results.
- Separate students into small groups to create their surveys. Read the steps aloud and draw students' attention to the topics box.
- Tell students to agree on a topic for their survey. If possible, try to get each group to do a different topic.
- When students begin step 4, draw their attention to the different graphs on page 121 and encourage them to use these kinds of visuals in their reports.

4 Now present the results of your survey to the class.
Groups complete the sentences about their surveys and present their surveys and results to the class. If there is extra time, allow the class to ask questions after each presentation.

> **The Digital Touch**
> To incorporate digital media in the project, suggest one or more of the following:
> - Students can create their charts in Excel or Google Sheets.
> - Students can create their presentations in PowerPoint or in Google Slides.
>
> Note that students should have the option to do a task on paper or digitally.

Wrap-up
Ask students to reflect on what they found out in their surveys and presentations. Ask *What surprised you? What didn't surprise you?* Elicit answers from the class.

 **Workbook p. 156, Activity 1 (Review)**

> **Teaching Tip**
> **Managing Choice and Variety**
> If possible, try to get each group to choose a different topic for their surveys. This will help keep things interesting when they present their results, and will avoid repetition.

 **Review**

Objective
Students will be able to consolidate their understanding of the vocabulary and grammar learned in the unit.

Lesson 11   Student's Book p. 122

> ✔ **Homework Check!**
> Workbook page 156, Activity 1 (Review)
> **Answers**
> **1 In your notebook, answer the questions.**
> Answers will vary.

Warm-up

Students review vocabulary for actions by acting out the different activities. Ask students to guess the word.

1 Match the parts.
Students match the parts of the phrases to create collocations for actions.

Answers
1. your room, 2. the dishes, 3. the dog, 4. the trash, 5. to the park, 6. friends, 7. video games, 8. a movie

2 Number the pictures using the phrases from Activity 1.
Students label photos by numbering them.

Answers
left to right, top to bottom 8, 1, 2, 4, 6, 7, 5, 3

3 Label the emoticons.
Students write the adjective that matches each emoticon.

Answers
1. nervous, 2. bored, 3. happy, 4. scared, 5. angry, 6. tired, 7. excited, 8. sad

Wrap-up

Students review emotion adjectives.
- Write the following sentence stems on the board:
    » *When I walk the dog, I feel…*
    » *When I clean my room, I feel…*
    » *When I hang out with friends, I feel…*
    » *When I play video games, I feel…*
- Tell students to use emotions adjectives to complete the sentences and write them in their notebooks.
- Then have students call out their answers and write them on the board.
- Have the class vote for each answer to see how many students agree with each adjective choice.

➡ **(No homework today.)**

Lesson 12   Student's Book p. 123

Warm-up

Students review the use of *have to* and *going to* by completing sentences.

- Write the following sentences on the board with gaps:
  Mike and Tim _____ study for their test. (have to)
  Regina _____ go to bed early tonight. (have to)
  Tom _____ go to France next month. (going to)
  Lisa and Jessica _____ study for their test at the library. (going to)
- Have students complete the sentences with the verbs in parentheses in their notebooks. Elicit answers from the class.

Answers
have to, has to, is going to, are going to

4 Complete the sentences with *have to* or *has to*. Then say the sentences.

Students complete the sentences with the correct form of *have to*. Invite volunteers to read the sentences aloud to the class.

Answers
1. have to, 2. has to, 3. has to, 4. have to, 5. have to, 6. has to

5 Write sentences using *be going to*.

Students use *going to* to write sentences using cues.

Answers
1. My grandmother is going to go to the park tomorrow., 2. Ben is going to watch a movie tonight., 3. The students are going to visit a museum next week., 4. Sarah and I are going to do the dishes after dinner., 5. I'm / I am going to clean my room on Saturday morning., 6. You're / You are going to take out the trash after lunch.

6 Unscramble the questions.

Students unscramble the questions using *going to*.

Answers
1. What are you going to do on the weekend?, 2. When are you going to go on vacation?, 3. Are you going to do your homework tonight?

7 In your notebook, answer the questions in Activity 6.

Students write sentences answering the questions they wrote in the previous activity using *going to*.

Answers
Answers will vary.

 Big Question

Students are given the opportunity to revisit the Big Question and reflect on it.

- Ask students to turn to the unit opener on page 111 and look at the question, *How do we spend our free time?*
- Have students work in small groups. Ask them to discuss the question based on their work in this unit.
- Tell students to think about the activities they have read about in this unit and the surveys they conducted in Lesson 10.
- Ask students to think about the time they spend doing things they *have to* do and the things they enjoy doing in their free time. Remind them of the emotions they associated with different activities. Ask *Are you happy with how you spend your free time? What would you do differently?*

Scorecard

Hand out (and/or project) a *Scorecard*. Have students fill in their *Scorecards* for this unit.

➡ **Study for the unit test.**

CD1 and CD2 Contents

CD 1

Worksheets

- **Grammar Worksheets**
  - Stopwatch 2 Answer Key Grammar.pdf
  - Stopwatch 2 Unit 0 Grammar 1 (2.0.G1).pdf
  - Stopwatch 2 Unit 0 Grammar 2 (2.0.G2).pdf
  - Stopwatch 2 Unit 0 Grammar 3 (2.0.G3).pdf
  - Stopwatch 2 Unit 0 Grammar 4 (2.0.G4).pdf
  - Stopwatch 2 Unit 0 Grammar 5 (2.0.G5).pdf
  - Stopwatch 2 Unit 0 Grammar 6 (2.0.G6).pdf
  - Stopwatch 2 Unit 1 Grammar 1 (2.1.G1).pdf
  - Stopwatch 2 Unit 1 Grammar 2 (2.1.G2).pdf
  - Stopwatch 2 Unit 2 Grammar 1 (2.2.G1).pdf
  - Stopwatch 2 Unit 2 Grammar 2 (2.2.G2).pdf
  - Stopwatch 2 Unit 3 Grammar 1 (2.3.G1).pdf
  - Stopwatch 2 Unit 3 Grammar 2 (2.3.G2).pdf
  - Stopwatch 2 Unit 4 Grammar 1 (2.4.G1).pdf
  - Stopwatch 2 Unit 4 Grammar 2 (2.4.G2).pdf
  - Stopwatch 2 Unit 5 Grammar 1 (2.5.G1).pdf
  - Stopwatch 2 Unit 5 Grammar 2 (2.5.G2).pdf
  - Stopwatch 2 Unit 6 Grammar 1 (2.6.G1).pdf
  - Stopwatch 2 Unit 6 Grammar 2 (2.6.G2).pdf
  - Stopwatch 2 Unit 7 Grammar 1 (2.7.G1).pdf
  - Stopwatch 2 Unit 7 Grammar 2 (2.7.G2).pdf
  - Stopwatch 2 Unit 8 Grammar 1 (2.8.G1).pdf
  - Stopwatch 2 Unit 8 Grammar 2 (2.8.G2).pdf
- **Reading Worksheets**
  - Stopwatch 2 Answer Key Reading.pdf
  - Stopwatch 2 Unit 1 Reading 1 (2.1.R1).pdf
  - Stopwatch 2 Unit 1 Reading 2 (2.1.R2).pdf
  - Stopwatch 2 Unit 2 Reading 1 (2.2.R1).pdf
  - Stopwatch 2 Unit 2 Reading 2 (2.2.R2).pdf
  - Stopwatch 2 Unit 3 Reading 1 (2.3.R1).pdf
  - Stopwatch 2 Unit 3 Reading 2 (2.3.R2).pdf
  - Stopwatch 2 Unit 4 Reading 1 (2.4.R1).pdf
  - Stopwatch 2 Unit 4 Reading 2 (2.4.R2).pdf
  - Stopwatch 2 Unit 5 Reading 1 (2.5.R1).pdf
  - Stopwatch 2 Unit 5 Reading 2 (2.5.R2).pdf
  - Stopwatch 2 Unit 6 Reading 1 (2.6.R1).pdf
  - Stopwatch 2 Unit 6 Reading 2 (2.6.R2).pdf
  - Stopwatch 2 Unit 7 Reading 1 (2.7.R1).pdf
  - Stopwatch 2 Unit 7 Reading 2 (2.7.R2).pdf
  - Stopwatch 2 Unit 8 Reading 1 (2.8.R1).pdf
  - Stopwatch 2 Unit 8 Reading 2 (2.8.R2).pdf
  - Stopwatch Reading Worksheets Guidelines.pdf
- **Vocabulary Worksheets**
  - Stopwatch 2 Answer Key Vocabulary.pdf
  - Stopwatch 2 Unit 1 Vocabulary 1 (2.1.V1).pdf
  - Stopwatch 2 Unit 1 Vocabulary 2 (2.1.V2).pdf
  - Stopwatch 2 Unit 2 Vocabulary 1 (2.2.V1).pdf
  - Stopwatch 2 Unit 2 Vocabulary 2 (2.2.V2).pdf
  - Stopwatch 2 Unit 3 Vocabulary 1 (2.3.V1).pdf
  - Stopwatch 2 Unit 3 Vocabulary 2 (2.3.V2).pdf
  - Stopwatch 2 Unit 4 Vocabulary 1 (2.4.V1).pdf
  - Stopwatch 2 Unit 4 Vocabulary 2 (2.4.V2).pdf
  - Stopwatch 2 Unit 5 Vocabulary 1 (2.5.V1).pdf
  - Stopwatch 2 Unit 5 Vocabulary 2 (2.5.V2).pdf
  - Stopwatch 2 Unit 6 Vocabulary 1 (2.6.V1).pdf
  - Stopwatch 2 Unit 6 Vocabulary 2 (2.6.V2).pdf
  - Stopwatch 2 Unit 7 Vocabulary 1 (2.7.V1).pdf
  - Stopwatch 2 Unit 7 Vocabulary 2 (2.7.V2).pdf
  - Stopwatch 2 Unit 8 Vocabulary 1 (2.8.V1).pdf
  - Stopwatch 2 Unit 8 Vocabulary 2 (2.8.V2).pdf

Class Audio CD 1
- Track 1—Track 34

CD 2

- **Project Rubrics**
  - Stopwatch 2 Project Rubrics.pdf
- **Scorecard**
  - Stopwatch 2 Scorecard.pdf
- **Test**
  - **Final Test**
    - Stopwatch 2 Answer Key Final Test.pdf
    - Stopwatch 2 Final Test.indd.pdf
  - **Mid-Term Test**
    - Stopwatch 2 Answer Key Mid-Term Exam.pdf
    - Stopwatch 2 Mid-Term Test.indd.pdf
  - **Placement Test**
    - Stopwatch Placement Test Answer Key.pdf
    - Stopwatch Placement Test.pdf
  - **Standard Tests**
    - Stopwatch 2 Answer Key Standard Test.pdf
    - Stopwatch 2 Standard Test U1.pdf
    - Stopwatch 2 Standard Test U2.pdf
    - Stopwatch 2 Standard Test U3.pdf
    - Stopwatch 2 Standard Test U4.pdf
    - Stopwatch 2 Standard Test U5.pdf
    - Stopwatch 2 Standard Test U6.pdf
    - Stopwatch 2 Standard Test U7.pdf
    - Stopwatch 2 Standard Test U8.pdf
  - **Test Plus**
    - Stopwatch 2 Answer Key Test Plus.pdf
    - Stopwatch 2 Test Plus U1.pdf
    - Stopwatch 2 Test Plus U2.pdf
    - Stopwatch 2 Test Plus U3.pdf
    - Stopwatch 2 Test Plus U4.pdf
    - Stopwatch 2 Test Plus U5.pdf
    - Stopwatch 2 Test Plus U6.pdf
    - Stopwatch 2 Test Plus U7.pdf
    - Stopwatch 2 Test Plus U8.pdf

Test Audio CD 2
- Track 1—Track 8 Unit Tests
- Track 9 Mid-Term
- Track 10 Final Test

Verb List Irregular verbs

Present Simple – Past simple

be – was / were
begin – began
break – broke
build – built
buy – bought
choose – chose
come – came
do – did
draw – drew
drive – drove
eat – ate
fall – fell
feel – felt
find – found
fly – flew
get – got
give – gave
go – went
grow – grew
have – had
hear – heard
know – knew
leave – left
lose – lost
make – made
meet – met
pay – paid
read – read
run – ran
see – saw
sing – sang
speak – spoke
swim – swam
take – took
teach – taught
tell – told
think – thought
wear – wore
win – won

Study Lists

Completely irregular
be – was / were
go – went

With an o in past
break – broke
choose – chose
drive – drove
get – got
lose – lost
speak – spoke
tell – told
wear – wore
win – won

With a long –ew sound in past
fly – flew
grow – grew
draw – drew
know – knew

With a short e sound in past
fall – fell
feel – felt
leave – left
meet – met

Ending in –ought / –aught in past
buy – bought
teach – taught
think – thought

i becomes a
begin – began
give – gave
sing – sang
swim – swam

Long a sound in past
come – came
eat – ate
make – made
pay – paid

The others
build – built
do – did
find – found
have – had
hear – heard
read – read
run – ran
see – saw
take – took